WIMBLEDON
2016

IN PURSUIT *of* GREATNESS

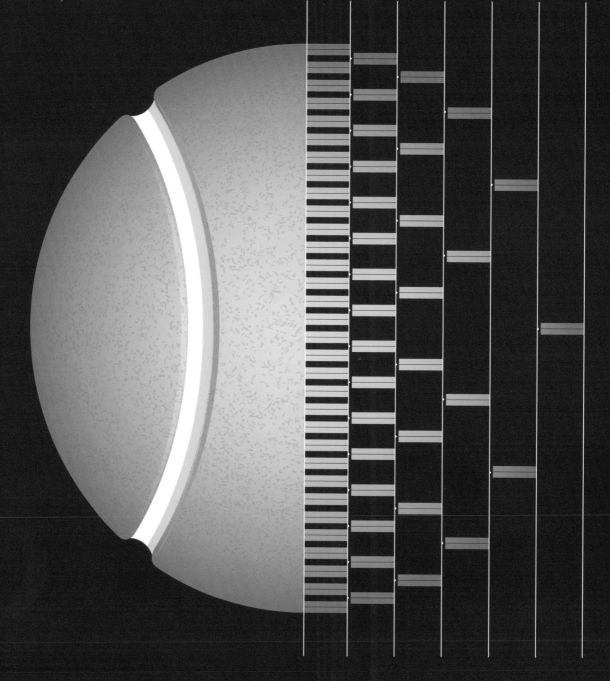

**THE CHAMPIONSHIPS
WIMBLEDON
27 JUNE — 10 JULY 2016**

**WIMBLEDON.COM
#WIMBLEDON**

The Official Poster 2016, designed by Brazilian artist Fernando Degrossi

WIMBLEDON
2016

By Paul Newman

ROLEX

Published in 2016 by Vision Sports Publishing Ltd

Vision Sports Publishing Ltd
19-23 High Street, Kingston upon Thames
Surrey, KT1 1LL
www.visionsp.co.uk

ISBN: 978-1909534-63-6

Written by: Paul Newman
Additional writing by: Ian Chadband
Edited by: Jim Drewett and Alexandra Willis
Production editors: Paul Baillie-Lane and Ed Davis
Designed by: Neal Cobourne
Photography: Bob Martin, Thomas Lovelock, Ben Queenborough, David Levenson, Eddie Keogh, Florian Eisele, Gary Hershorn, Jed Leicester, Joe Toth, Joel Marklund, Jon Buckle, Karwai Tang, Paul Gregory, Richard Washbrooke, Roger Allen, Samuel Bay, Simon Lodge, Steve Lewis
Picture research: Paul Weaver, Neil Turner and Sarah Frandsen

All photographs © AELTC

Results and tables are reproduced courtesy of the AELTC

The All England Lawn Tennis Club (Championships) Limited
Church Road, Wimbledon, London, SW19 5AE, England
Tel: +44 (0)20 8944 1066
Fax: +44 (0)20 8947 8752
www.wimbledon.com

Printed in Slovakia by Neografia

This book is reproduced with the assistance of Rolex.

CONTENTS

FOREWORD
by Chairman Philip Brook

The Championships 2016 will be remembered for many things.

Firstly, the weather, which after years of being kind to us finally changed its mind. After 113 consecutive days of play without a rain refund (almost nine years), our streak was broken. But the showers of the first week gave way to the sunshine of the second week, and we still saw some wonderful weather.

We added singles to our wheelchair tennis events, something we were pleased and proud to do, and were delighted to witness British success in those events, with Gordon Reid winning the Gentlemen's Singles and Doubles titles, the latter alongside Alfie Hewett, and Jordanne Whiley defending her Ladies' Doubles title.

We enjoyed the occasion of Middle Saturday, as Centre Court rose to salute Joy Lofthouse, a former Second World War Spitfire pilot, who outstripped even David Beckham for applause. Thank you to Joy and to all the members of the Armed Forces who play such an important role at Wimbledon.

And we had Middle Sunday for only the fourth time in the history of The Championships and the first since we've had a roof. Times have changed since the last Middle Sunday in 2004, with an online ticket sale which had over 111,000 applicants and sold out in 27 minutes. I would like to thank all those behind the scenes who gave up their Sunday and worked tirelessly to give over 22,000 people the opportunity to visit Wimbledon, many of them for the first time, and enjoy an excellent day of tennis.

We also said 'goodbye' to Court 19, which hosted its last match, a girls' doubles on Friday evening. It will become part of a three-year construction project which will see the addition of a retractable roof on No. 1 Court.

Congratulations to all of our champions, in particular to Andy Murray, three times a Wimbledon finalist, and now twice a Wimbledon champion, and to Serena Williams, a Ladies' Singles champion here for an incredible seventh time, also taking her tally of Grand Slam singles titles to 22, equalling Steffi Graf's record. Not content with one title, Serena returned to the court alongside sister Venus to win the Ladies' Doubles title, their sixth together here at Wimbledon, another extraordinary achievement. And to Heather Watson, the first British Mixed Doubles champion since Jamie Murray's success with Jelena Jankovic in 2007.

Finally, our thanks go to all those who attended or engaged with The Championships. Despite the distractions of the referendum, the European Football Championship and other events on the global stage, the eyes of the world remained on Wimbledon. I hope this annual will prove to be a memorable and enjoyable read.

Philip Brook

WHEN YOUR TRADITIONS ARE KNOWN TO ALL, YOU'VE MADE HISTORY.

This watch is a witness to epic battles on Centre Court. Worn on the wrists of those who have made Wimbledon's traditions great. It doesn't just tell time. It tells history.

OYSTER PERPETUAL DATEJUST 41

ROLEX

LADIES DOUBLES

MIXED DOUBLES

Robin HAASE
Andreas SEPPI
Guillermo GARCIA-LOPEZ
Pablo CARRENO BUSTA
Milos RAONIC
Roger FEDERER
Guido PELLA
Ricardas BERANKIS
Marcus WILLIS
Daniel EVANS

INTRODUCTION
By Paul Newman

t often amuses overseas visitors to hear how much the British talk about the weather. However, those who visited Britain – or indeed almost anywhere in western Europe – in the spring and early summer of 2016 would have left with a better understanding of one of our national obsessions.

In many regions the weather was, to be blunt, dreadful, with sometimes record-breaking levels of rain. It was often unpredictable and frequently localised. Who would have imagined that in the first week of June the Manchester grass court tournament would bask in glorious sunshine in a city which has long been the recipient of jokes about its high rainfall, while the second week of the French Open in Paris would be played out in shivering temperatures under rain-filled skies?

For most of us, bad weather can be an inconvenience. For the organisers of outdoor tennis events, it can be a nightmare. As the new tournament director at the French Open, Guy Forget had a baptism of fire (perhaps not the most appropriate phrase in the circumstances) after one of the wettest Mays in living memory in Paris, where the rainfall was three times higher than average and the Seine burst its banks. On the opening Monday at Roland Garros a whole day's play was lost for the first time in 16 years.

If rain can be a problem on clay, where the surface can become heavy and slippery, playing tennis on wet grass is impossible. With rain continuing to fall throughout June it was remarkable that all the grass court tournaments in Britain in the build-up to The Championships finished on time, though the men's final in Surbiton had to be completed indoors. As The Championships approached there was little sign of improvement as rain disrupted the qualifying competition at Roehampton, the tournaments in Eastbourne and Nottingham and practice for everyone. The rainfall in the counties of Surrey and Middlesex in June was more than twice the average for the month.

It was just as well that The Championships now sit a week later in the calendar than they did until 2015. With three weeks instead of two to hone their grass court game after the French Open,

the players still had time to adjust to the change of surface, although the defending singles champions, Novak Djokovic and Serena Williams, stuck to their recent tried and tested formula of not playing any competitive tennis in the build-up.

The early weeks of the season were not without surprises. Roger Federer, having missed the French Open because of a back problem, was beaten in Stuttgart and Halle by Dominic Thiem and Alexander Zverev respectively, which inevitably led to headlines about a changing of the guard. However, both young tyros went on to lose in Halle to the eventual champion, 32-year-old Florian Mayer, who was ranked No.192 in the world after a year of injury problems.

Meanwhile Stan Wawrinka was beaten by Fernando Verdasco in his only competitive grass court encounter before The Championships, Agnieszka Radwanska lost her opening match to Coco Vandeweghe and Garbiñe Muguruza, runner-up at The Championships in 2015, went down to Kirsten Flipkens in her first match at the inaugural Mallorca Open, barely a week after winning her maiden Grand Slam title at the French Open.

At the Aegon Championships at The Queen's Club, nevertheless, it was business as usual for Andy Murray in his first week back with his coach, Ivan Lendl. Murray, who had just reached his first French Open final before losing to the all-conquering Djokovic, became the first man to win the historic title (and trophy) five times after an enthralling battle in the final with Milos Raonic, who had recruited John McEnroe to his coaching team.

And so to Wimbledon. The cover of last year's edition of this book had described The Championships 2015 as "a year of glorious weather and even more glorious tennis". On the evidence so far, 2016 would struggle to live up to the first part of that description, but there was every prospect of a repeat of the second, even if Rafael Nadal, twice a champion, and Victoria Azarenka, one of the year's most successful players, would be missing through injury. It was time to find out.

Far right: No.1 Court comes under a deluge in the week preceding The Championships

Below: Nice weather for ducks! The qualifying tournament at the Bank of England Sports Centre in Roehampton was severely disrupted

Fun and games

The unusually wet weather couldn't put a dampener on the mood in the week prior to The Championships as the players gathered in London, SW19, to hit a few balls, get used to the grass again and generally hang out with each other. This was the second year that the stars of tennis had enjoyed an extra week to prepare for Wimbledon following the conclusion of the French Open and, judging by the smiling faces, the long-awaited amendment to the schedule has gone down well.

WIMBLEDON 2016
Gentlemen's Singles Seeds

Novak DJOKOVIC ❶
(Serbia)
Age: 29

Wimbledon titles: 3 | Grand Slam titles: 12

Andy MURRAY ❷
(Great Britain)
Age: 29

Wimbledon titles: 1 | Grand Slam titles: 2

Roger FEDERER ❸
(Switzerland)
Age: 34

Wimbledon titles: 7 | Grand Slam titles: 17

Stan WAWRINKA ❹
(Switzerland)
Age: 31

Wimbledon titles: 0 | Grand Slam titles: 2

Kei NISHIKORI ❺
(Japan)
Age: 26

Wimbledon titles: 0 | Grand Slam titles: 0

Milos RAONIC ❻
(Canada)
Age: 25

Wimbledon titles: 0 | Grand Slam titles: 0

Richard GASQUET ❼
(France)
Age: 30

Wimbledon titles: 0 | Grand Slam titles: 0

Dominic THIEM ❽
(Austria)
Age: 22

Wimbledon titles: 0 | Grand Slam titles: 0

Marin CILIC (Croatia) ❾

Tomas BERDYCH (Czech Republic) ❿

David GOFFIN (Belgium) ⓫

Jo-Wilfried TSONGA (France) ⓬

David FERRER (Spain) ⓭

Roberto BAUTISTA AGUT (Spain) ⓮

Nick KYRGIOS (Australia) ⓯

Gilles SIMON (France) ⓰

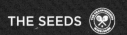

Ladies' Singles Seeds

Serena WILLIAMS ❶
(USA)
Age: 34
Wimbledon titles: 6 | Grand Slam titles: 21

Garbiñe MUGURUZA ❷
(Spain)
Age: 22
Wimbledon titles: 0 | Grand Slam titles: 1

Agnieszka RADWANSKA ❸
(Poland)
Age: 27
Wimbledon titles: 0 | Grand Slam titles: 0

Angelique KERBER ❹
(Germany)
Age: 28
Wimbledon titles: 0 | Grand Slam titles: 1

Simona HALEP ❺
(Romania)
Age: 24
Wimbledon titles: 0 | Grand Slam titles: 0

Roberta VINCI ❻
(Italy)
Age: 33
Wimbledon titles: 0 | Grand Slam titles: 0

Belinda BENCIC ❼
(Switzerland)
Age: 19
Wimbledon titles: 0 | Grand Slam titles: 0

Venus WILLIAMS ❽
(USA)
Age: 36
Wimbledon titles: 5 | Grand Slam titles: 7

Madison KEYS (USA) ❾
Petra KVITOVA (Czech Republic) ❿
Timea BACSINSZKY (Switzerland) ⓫
Carla SUAREZ NAVARRO (Spain) ⓬

Svetlana KUZNETSOVA (Russia) ⓭
Samantha STOSUR (Australia) ⓮
Karolina PLISKOVA (Czech Republic) ⓯
Johanna KONTA (Great Britain) ⓰

DAY
1

MONDAY
27 JUNE

As the 130th edition of The Championships got under way the weather was not the only aspect of British life that looked unsettled. While the opening day at the All England Club actually brought some of the best weather of the first week, there could be no mistaking the feeling of uncertainty in the air after the country had voted just four days earlier to leave the European Union.

It was a referendum result that had surprised many, including plenty of those in the pro-'Brexit' camp. As thousands of tennis fans headed for Wimbledon there was probably as much talk among them about the country's future as there was of Andy Murray's chances of winning a second Wimbledon title or of Serena Williams winning her seventh.

Since the announcement of the referendum result, British politics had been in turmoil. The Prime Minister, David Cameron, having headed the 'Remain' campaign, had promptly announced his resignation. By Monday the election of a new leader appeared to be a two-horse race between Boris Johnson, who had been a focal point of the 'Leave' campaign, and Theresa May, the Home Secretary. Meanwhile the opposition Labour Party was also in ferment as 11 senior members of the Shadow Cabinet, unhappy with Jeremy Corbyn's leadership during the campaign, resigned.

In such troubled times it can take a sporting triumph to revive a country's spirits. Wales and England were still in football's European Championship, which was being staged in France, but England had not impressed and were facing a potential banana skin against Iceland that very evening. Could Britain's tennis players step up to the challenge instead?

The early signs were not encouraging. Kyle Edmund, who at 21 is considered Britain's brightest male prospect, was one of the day's first losers, going down 2-6, 5-7, 4-6 to France's Adrian Mannarino on No.2 Court. It was surely too much to hope that James Ward would fare any better against Novak Djokovic as the world No.1 began the defence of his title in the opening match on Centre Court. Ward, who had gone through a difficult period after the untimely death of his coach, Darren Tandy, at the end of the previous year, lost the first nine games after making what he later called an "ugly start". The world No.177, making his first appearance on Centre Court, nevertheless made a fight of it thereafter and had three break points at 5-5 in the second set before Djokovic completed his 6-0, 7-6(3), 6-4 victory. The 29-year-old Serb, playing his first competitive match since completing a 'career Grand Slam' by winning the French Open three weeks earlier, thought he had let his concentration slip at times but added: "The first part of the match was almost flawless, so I'm very pleased with the way I started Wimbledon."

If Edmund and Ward, two heroes of Britain's triumphant Davis Cup team the previous year, could not provide one of the wins that home supporters craved, how about one of the leading lights from the Coventry and District Lawn Tennis League? Marcus Willis, the world No.772, had lit up the qualifying tournament for The Championships the previous week with some remarkable performances, winning three matches against significantly higher-ranked opponents to secure a place in the main draw of a Grand Slam event for the first time. Before that he had had to take time off from his coaching job at Warwick Boat Club to play in a British pre-qualifying competition, in which he won three matches to earn a wild card into the qualifying event. He had got into pre-qualifying only because a higher-ranked player could not get back in time from an overseas competition.

Marcus Willis celebrates victory with his ecstatic supporters – mostly his friends from university – following his stunning first day win

Having won a total of six matches just to reach the main draw, Willis was determined to extend his run, which he did with a stunning 6-3, 6-3, 6-4 victory over Lithuania's Ricardas Berankis, who was ranked 718 places higher than his opponent. Cheered on by a raucous group of supporters on Court 17, Willis bewildered the world No.54 with his combination of big serves, confident volleys and unorthodox ground strokes, which he struck with a clever mix of different speeds and spins. He showed great mental resilience too, saving 19 out of 20 break points. After the match his boyhood hero, Goran Ivanisevic, the 2001 Wimbledon champion, sought him out to shake his hand. Two days later, incredibly, Willis would be shaking hands with Roger Federer, who would be his second-round opponent.

At his post-match press conference Willis talked more about his extraordinary story. As a junior he had shown great promise, but in his teenage years his commitment and attitude failed to match his talent. In 2008 he was sent home from the Australian Open junior event by the Lawn Tennis Association because of his lackadaisical attitude, which was typified when he arrived late at a practice session without his rackets, having left them at the hotel. "When I was a junior, I was talented," Willis said. "I was bigged up a lot. Then I got dropped in the real world. I played Futures in Romania, losing, and lost a lot of confidence. I made some bad decisions. I went out too much. My lifestyle wasn't good. I didn't have the drive."

It was not until he was 22 that Willis discovered that drive. "I was a bit of a loser," he said when asked what had brought about the change of attitude. "I was overweight. I was seeing off pints. I was just a loser. I just looked myself in the mirror and said: 'You're better than this'."

Willis, who lives with his parents in Berkshire, reached a career-high position at No.322 in the world rankings in 2014, but making a living at that level of tennis was all but impossible. "I played a tournament in Spain, won the singles and then lost the final in the doubles," he recalled. "My profit was 60 euros."

Wimbledon's popular Service Stewards – volunteers from the British Army, Royal Navy and Royal Air Force – always add to the colour and atmosphere of The Championships

Shoes off to him!

We will not forget Marcus Willis and his fabulous fans in a hurry. It all started in a corner pocket of the outpost that is Court 17 as a comical racket began to emerge and, around the Grounds, it dawned that one of the great Wimbledon fairytales was unfolding.

Willis, the most unlikely of qualifiers ranked No.772 in the world, was pulling off a sensation against Lithuania's world No.54, Ricardas Berankis, with each of his winning points being accompanied by a rich variety of daft chants from a small bunch of Marcus's buddies in the crowd.

The weirdest refrain from the crew calling themselves 'the Willbombs' was "Shoes off if you love Willis!", at which point they took off said footwear and waved them in the air. Suitably encouraged, a whole host of well-shod spectators did likewise at courtside, laughing heartily at the crazy nature of it all.

Even the happy-go-lucky Willis joined in the fun, picking up a spare trainer at one of the changeovers and hoisting it above his head. "Joined along with it," he smiled. "It's a bit surreal, so I thought I might as well enjoy it."

Not that his opponent looked too thrilled at the adaptation of the '90s dance favourite 'Freed from Desire' – brought back into the

Sole mates! The Marcus Willis Fan Club lit up Court 17 with their humorous antics. By the end of the match, even onlookers from the Debenture Holders' balcony were removing their footwear in acclaim of Britain's unlikeliest tennis hero

public consciousness thanks to Northern Ireland's fans serenading their striker Will Grigg with it at the European Championship – that Willis' supporters happily crooned: "Berankis is terrified, Willbomb's on fire!"

At the end, the victorious Willis was buried in a scrum of his chums and paid tribute to the most infectious barmy army Wimbledon had probably ever seen.

"They're actually tennis players as well," he said. "Been my friends for a long time. Guys from Loughborough Uni as well, have been watching me through qualies. Thanks to them, they made it a great atmosphere out there."

Next stop, Centre Court. Altogether now: "Federer is terrified…"

That summer Willis set up a pledge website page to raise money to fund his career, saying his goal was to play at Wimbledon the following year. He raised £2,185. By the end of 2015, nevertheless, he was ready to throw in the towel. "I had a really bad Christmas," he admitted.

In January 2016 Willis played in a Futures tournament in Tunisia, where he won two matches in singles and one in doubles, which earned total prize money of just $354. That was his last appearance before Wimbledon. "I'd had enough," he said. "I had no money. I didn't get out of bed. I was really down."

However, Willis enjoyed his coaching work and was considering taking up a coaching post in Philadelphia when his new girlfriend, Jennifer Bate, persuaded him to have another crack at a playing career. "I did what I was told," Willis said.

By reaching the second round Willis had guaranteed himself a pay cheque of £50,000, which would almost double his total career earnings. His next opponent, meanwhile, had earned prize money totalling nearly $100m. Asked to compare his game with Federer's, Willis replied with a smile: "Is his game just a little bit better than mine? I didn't think I'd be answering these questions in a million years. He's a complete player, a legend of the game."

After a terrible time with injury, Laura Robson was unfortunate to be drawn against Australian Open champion Angelique Kerber, who beat her 6-2, 6-2

Federer, who showed no signs of the back problem which had forced him to miss the French Open as he began his 18th consecutive campaign at The Championships with a 7-6(5), 7-6(3), 6-3 victory over Argentina's Guido Pella, said he had been following Willis' progress with great interest. "I think it's been one of the best stories in our sport for a long time," he said. "These are the kind of stories we need in our sport. I'm very excited to be playing him."

Willis was not the only British winner on the opening day. Dan Evans, playing in the main draw of a Grand Slam tournament by dint of his world ranking for the first time, beat Germany's Jan-Lennard Struff 6-3, 6-7(6), 7-6(7), 7-5 to earn a second-round meeting with Alexandr Dolgopolov. However, Brydan Klein and Alex Ward lost to Nicolas Mahut and David Goffin respectively, while the two Britons in action in the Ladies' Singles also went out. Laura Robson, continuing to struggle in her comeback following wrist surgery, lost 2-6, 2-6 to Angelique Kerber, the Australian Open champion, and Naomi Broady was beaten 2-6, 3-6 by Ukraine's Elina Svitolina.

On a day which saw the departure of four men's seeds – Gael Monfils, Kevin Anderson, Philipp Kohlschreiber and Pablo Cuevas – Kei Nishikori saw off the big-serving Sam Groth while Milos Raonic eased to a straight-sets victory over Pablo Carreno Busta.

Irina-Camelia Begu of Romania had the unwanted distinction of being the first seed to go out when she was beaten 1-6, 4-6 by Germany's Carina Witthoeft. Ana Ivanovic, the former French Open champion, also fell at the first hurdle, having suffered with a wrist injury during her 2-6, 5-7 defeat by Russian qualifier Ekaterina Alexandrova. Nineteen years after making her debut at The Championships, 36-year-old Venus Williams reached the second round by beating 19-year-old Donna Vekic 7-6(3), 6-4.

Novak's towel secret

Novak Djokovic "loses himself" in a Wimbledon towel

● **Novak Djokovic's guilty secret** popped out after he began the defence of his Gentlemen's Singles title with a routine first-round triumph over Britain's James Ward.

Asked afterwards about the famous Wimbledon towels given to the players during matches, the champ began to wax lyrical. "[They're] my comfort zone, let's say. For a second or two, I'm able to lose myself in a towel if I need some concentration. The size of the towel is perfect for that."

They also happened to be in such demand among his friends as souvenirs, he explained, that he would simply use the excuse that "it's too warm and I'm sweating" to "sneak" an extra towel into his tennis bag.

"I'm sure the All England Club Committee will forgive me for that extra towel per match," he said, a mite pleadingly. Of course, you're forgiven Novak – as long as you don't mind from now on being known as Wimbledon's Raffles, the gentlemanly towel thief of SW19!

● **Garbiñe Muguruza cut a dash** on the eve of the tournament, delighting photographers when she wandered around the All England Club in a replica Spanish football kit to show her support for the team competing at the European Championship in France.

Unfortunately, it didn't bring her boys much luck, though. On the Monday, while the 2015 finalist was beating Italian Camila Giorgi on Centre Court, another Spain-Italy clash was being played out in Paris and by the time Muguruza emerged victorious, she was a bit deflated to discover that Spain had lost 2-0 to the Azzurri.

There was better news on the football cheerleading front for Australian Open champ Angelique Kerber, who revealed that she

Garbiñe Muguruza sports her Spain football top

had prepared for her first-round tie with Britain's Laura Robson by cheering Germany to a 3-0 victory over Slovakia in the last 16.

"It's nice to be supporting them... I'm jumping, screaming. Sometimes I'm quiet as well. A lot of emotions in these 90 minutes!" Kerber explained. It sounded exhausting – but she still had enough energy to beat Robson in straight sets.

● **A familiar face was back on Centre Court** as Sir Cliff Richard enjoyed the opening day's play. It brought back a few memories of 20 years earlier when one of Britain's biggest show business stars conducted his now fabled sing-along there, along with a backing supergroup that included Martina Navratilova and Virginia Wade.

Things have changed a little, though. With a roof now in place to ensure no interruptions to the tennis action, nobody, rather disappointingly, was about to ask 75-year-old Sir Cliff for a repeat booking.

IN PURSUIT *of* GREATNESS

In pursuit of greatness

Wimbledon is proud of what it has achieved, building a sporting event that is the envy of the world and striving to do things with honour, integrity and grace. Yet there is also a recognition of how the event could always be improved. 'In Pursuit of Greatness' has become its daily mission statement.

Take 'The List'. "It's something that begins during The Championships, a list of all the things that we can do better," explains AELTC Chief Executive Richard Lewis.

"It goes right to the heart of not accepting second best. If it's something that can't be dealt with immediately then it goes on 'The List'. Every single line has to have a comment by it by next year's Championships.

"The moment that you are satisfied and think that you can't improve on it, that's the moment when you've got a problem. We just want it to be better. Every day and every year."

DAY
2
TUESDAY
28 JUNE

COURT 19

M. Granollers	6 2	•40
V. Estrella Burgos	2 3	40

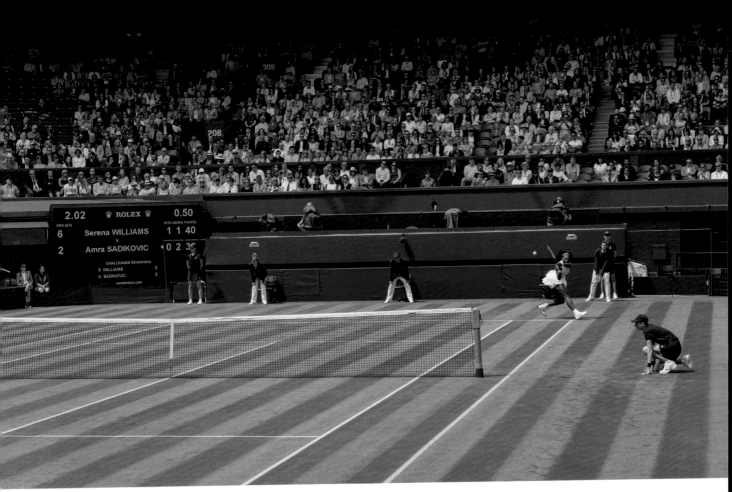

W hen Serena Williams left the All England Club at the end of The Championships 2015 her stock could hardly have been higher. In claiming her sixth Wimbledon title the world No.1 had completed her second 'Serena Slam' – holding all four Grand Slam titles at the same time – and was three-quarters of the way towards matching the feats of Maureen Connolly, Margaret Court and Steffi Graf by winning a pure calendar-year singles Grand Slam.

Above: 2015 Ladies' Singles champion Serena Williams began her quest for a record-equalling 22nd Grand Slam title against Switzerland's Amra Sadikovic

With a total of 21 Grand Slam titles to her name, it seemed certain that it would be only a matter of time before she would equal Graf's Open era record of 22. By anyone else's standards the next 12 months would have been exceptional, but nobody sets the bar higher than Williams. While it was still a major achievement to reach the semi-finals of the US Open and to finish runner-up at the Australian and French Opens, there was, inevitably, speculation as to how the American was coping with the pressures of making history. She had struggled to come to terms with her defeat to Roberta Vinci at Flushing Meadows to the extent that she did not play again until the following January, while the losses in Melbourne and Paris dented her remarkable record in Grand Slam finals. Until the start of 2016 she had won 21 of the 25 finals she had contested.

"You cannot play a Grand Slam final for history in the same way as any other," Patrick Mouratoglou, Williams' coach, had admitted after her defeat to Garbiñe Muguruza at Roland Garros. "This 22nd Grand Slam title is difficult."

Mouratoglou stressed, nevertheless, that he never discussed with the world No.1 the prospect of equalling Graf's record, while Williams herself insisted on the eve of The Championships: "Honestly, I don't feel any pressure. I feel good and confident."

By 1pm on the second day of The Championships it was time for actions to speak louder than words as Williams went on Centre Court to begin the defence of her title against Switzerland's Amra Sadikovic, the world No.148. Williams went 15-40 down in the first game but order was quickly restored. The American won the next 13 points to take a 3-0 lead and needed just 73 minutes to complete a 6-2, 6-4 victory. It was her 80th win in her 90th match at The Championships.

While Williams clearly had plenty of room for improvement on her serve – she hit only four aces and made five double faults – she was satisfied with her performance. "For a first round I felt I was where I needed to be," she said afterwards. "It was a good start." The American also insisted that she had always had the strength to deal with whatever challenges she had faced. "Mentally I've been further down than anyone can be," she said. "Well, maybe not anyone, but I've been pretty low. There's nothing that's not mentally too hard for me."

Caroline Wozniacki has also had to cope with highs and lows. Two years ago the former world No.1 reached her second US Open final before losing to Williams, but not much had gone right for her since. Wozniacki arrived at The Championships without a victory at a Grand Slam event in 2016, having lost to Yulia Putintseva at the Australian Open and missing the French Open because of an ankle injury. She had fallen to No.45 in the world rankings, meaning she would be unseeded at a Grand Slam tournament for the first time in eight years.

It was Wozniacki's misfortune to be drawn in the first round against Svetlana Kuznetsova, who was still going strong at 31. The No.13 seed won 7-5, 6-4, though she was pushed hard by Wozniacki, who had taken some encouragement from her form the previous week in Eastbourne, where she had won back-to-back matches for the first time in more than three months.

"It's been a tough year in general," Wozniacki said afterwards. "I've had some injuries, some bad draws. It's been uphill. But you just have to keep fighting, keep going at it, keep working hard, and hope eventually that it's going to turn and you're going to take the chances you're going to get."

Wozniacki and Kuznetsova played under the Centre Court roof after rain brought the first disruption to The Championships programme. Play never restarted on the other courts after rain started falling just after 4.30pm. The gloom seemed to match the nation's mood after the England football team's shocking defeat to Iceland the previous evening, which had prompted the immediate resignation of Roy Hodgson, the manager. The fact that Wales were still in the competition almost compounded English embarrassment.

Scotland were the only home nation not represented in France, though there were high hopes that the country's most celebrated sportsman would provide some cheer at The Championships. Andy Murray, who had begun the year by finishing runner-up at the Australian Open for the fifth time, had just enjoyed the most successful clay court season of his career by reaching the finals at Roland Garros and Madrid and

Top: Caroline Wozniacki's troubled 2016 continued with defeat to the powerful veteran Svetlana Kuznetsova **(above)**

Dressed to frill

With Wimbledon's 'predominantly white' rule on what players can and cannot wear being enforced more strictly than ever these days, the gauntlet is well and truly laid down to the sportswear manufacturers to come up with imaginative dress designs. For the 2016 Championships Garbiñe Muguruza *(below)* enlisted the help of renowned designer Stella McCartney, whilst Serena Williams *(right)* sported a slightly more frilly number, not the so-called Nike 'Nightie' that caused something of a stir around the Grounds. Modelled by the likes of Donna Vekic *(below, right)*, the unusual garment did have a tendency to rise up and flap around during play, as demonstrated by Britain's Katie Swan *(bottom)*. Some players, like Anna Schmiedlova *(below, far right)* even resorted to homemade alterations to keep their outfits under control.

winning the title in Rome. Not even a parting of the ways with Amelie Mauresmo, his coach of the previous two years, could halt his momentum. Indeed, after reuniting with Ivan Lendl, who had guided him to his previous two Grand Slam triumphs, Murray had won the title at The Queen's Club in their first tournament back together.

Until the Aegon Championships Murray had not played a fellow Briton at tour level since his three meetings with Tim Henman in 2006. However, after beating Aljaz Bedene and Kyle Edmund at Queen's, Murray was paired with a third Briton, Liam Broady, in the first round at The Championships. It was the first all-British men's match at the All England Club since 2001, when Henman beat Martin Lee in the second round, and the first at any Grand Slam tournament since the 2006 US Open, when Henman beat Greg Rusedski in the first round. Broady, aged 22, had been runner-up in the boys' singles at The Championships 2011 and had won the boys' doubles title alongside Tom Farquharson the previous year. He had also won on his Grand Slam singles debut in 2015, beating Marinko Matosevic before losing to David Goffin.

Having been taken to five sets in his first two matches at the French Open, Murray was keen not to expend too much energy in the early rounds here and he took just an hour and 42 minutes to win 6-2, 6-3, 6-4, completing his Centre Court victory just before the rain arrived.

"For a first match, to get it done in three sets is good," said Murray. "I hit the ball pretty cleanly today. I think offensively I was good. I felt like I could have moved a little bit better and I didn't defend as well as usual, but I served well, too. That was pleasing."

Broady, who improved as the match progressed, said: "I felt at home from the start. I didn't play like I was at home from the start, but I certainly felt like it. I think the longer the match went on, the more I focused on the tennis and stopped remembering where I was."

Bedene was beaten 3-6, 4-6, 3-6 by Richard Gasquet, while 17-year-old Katie Swan, making her Grand Slam debut, lost 2-6, 3-6 to Timea Babos. Johanna Konta, the British No.1, was leading Monica Puig 6-1, 2-1 when play was abandoned for the day.

Tara Moore was one of those who beat the weather, a 6-3, 6-2 victory over Alison Van Uytvanck giving the 23-year-old Briton her first success at Grand Slam level. At No.227 in the world Moore was ranked 100 places below her Belgian opponent, who had been a quarter-finalist at the French Open in 2015.

Moore earned a wild card into The Championships after making the final at Eastbourne and winning five matches in Nottingham to reach her first tour-level quarter-final. "Who would have thought before

Previous pages: Un-Wimbledon-like grey clouds provide the backdrop to Stan Wawrinka's first-round victory over Taylor Fritz on No.1 Court

Tara Moore **(below left)** flew the flag for Britain's ladies with victory over Alison Van Uytvanck to take her into the second round. Liam Broady **(below)** could not match her achievement but at least the man who beat him was also a Brit... a certain Andy Murray

You cannot be serious! Visitors on Day 2 were spluttering into their Pimm's in disbelief until they realised that the Borg and McEnroe wandering the Grounds all day were actually a pair of fun-loving Italian lookalikes

the grass season that I'd be where I am right now?" she said after beating Van Uytvanck. "I'm really grateful to the All England Club for giving me this opportunity. I think I've definitely worked really hard and I've definitely put in a lot of graft and I think it's paying off finally."

Nick Kyrgios came through what he described as a "nightmare" first-round draw to beat Radek Stepanek 6-4, 6-3, 6-7(9), 6-1. Kyrgios has become good friends with Stepanek and had talked about being coached by the 37-year-old Czech. By Kyrgios' standards the match was straightforward, though it featured one typically extravagant shot by the 21-year-old Australian – a winning through-the-legs lob – and a warning from the umpire about his language. The victory earned a second-round meeting with the equally flamboyant German, Dustin Brown, who beat Dusan Lajovic 4-6, 6-3, 3-6, 6-3, 6-4.

Arguably the most popular victory of the day saw Juan Martin del Potro beat France's Stephane Robert 6-1, 7-5, 6-0. The 27-year-old Argentinian, who was making his first appearance at The Championships in three years after undergoing three wrist operations, set up a heavyweight second-round showdown with Stan Wawrinka, who beat the youngest player in the draw, 18-year-old Taylor Fritz of the United States, 7-6(4), 6-1, 6-7(2), 6-4.

Kevin hits out at the haters

Kevin Anderson received some disturbing abuse on social media following his first round defeat

CHAMPIONSHIPS
Day
2
NOTEBOOK

● **Kevin Anderson, who came closest to beating Novak Djokovic** during his triumphant 2015 Wimbledon campaign, gave a hint of some of the more depressing aspects of the things the modern-day professional has to endure in the internet age after his first round five-set defeat by Uzbekistan's Denis Istomin.

The South African revealed to the BBC World Service that he had received "death threats" after the loss from people who had bet on the match. "It pretty much happens after every match regardless of the circumstances," Anderson explained. "It's just something you have to deal with as a professional athlete who is in the limelight.

"It would be nicer if you didn't have to put up with it, but that's the reality of the world we live in."

● **John McEnroe, who some reckon to be as good a commentator** as he was a player, found the perfect way of describing the task awaiting Amra Sadikovic as she faced defending champion Serena Williams in the opening round.

Having watched a certain footballing sensation unfold on British TV on the eve of the match, Supermac found the perfect analogy. "This is sort of like England playing Iceland. If Sadikovic wins, this would be even more monumental!" he said. Unlike victorious Iceland, though, the Swiss proved a fairly tame underdog.

● **Petr Cech, the brilliant Arsenal and Czech Republic goalkeeper**, is such a great pal of Radek Stepanek that, after the European Championship, he flew straight to London to support his friend at courtside during his opening round defeat to Nick Kyrgios.

Cech mate! Radek Stepanek's celebrity fan and ball boy

"I was supposed to be going to Italy for my holidays but I postponed it so I could see his first game," explained Cech. "Also, I went to act as his ball boy when he was practising at the weekend in a match with Lukas Rosol!" The worst part of his job as ball boy? Apparently, picking the ball out of the net was no fun...

● **As part of wimbledon.com's fascinating 'If' series**, in which top players were asked a series of questions at the start of The Championships, one of the most intriguing set of responses was to the poser: "If you could choose one person to play you in a movie..."

It generated splendid answers. Kei Nishikori saw himself being played by Orlando Bloom, Novak Djokovic chose Leonardo Di Caprio, Angelique Kerber went for Julia Roberts and Roger Federer thought Matt Damon would be ideal. The best response of all? Stan Wawrinka, who, a little tongue in cheek, suggested Denzel Washington would be perfect for the role.

DAY 3

WEDNESDAY 29 JUNE

Roger Federer had played 90 matches in the Gentlemen's Singles at The Championships dating back to his debut in 1999, but the seven-time champion had never faced a contest quite like this. On paper, the world No.3's second-round meeting with Britain's Marcus Willis, the world No.772, was one of the greatest mismatches in Wimbledon history.

On one side of the net was arguably the greatest player of all time, who had won more Grand Slam singles titles than any other man, earned nearly $100m in prize money and won 1,073 tour-level matches. On the other stood a club coach who had not played a tournament since a Futures event in Tunisia in January, had total career earnings of less than $100,000 and had played his first match at tour level just 48 hours earlier.

As they walked out on to Centre Court, Federer having insisted that his opponent should have the privilege of going first, Willis' kit spoke volumes of the gulf between the two men. The 25-year-old Briton was wearing a shirt bearing Federer's 'RF' logo which he had bought ahead of last year's qualifying competition for The Championships, though he had failed to make the starting line-up. "It's a bit weird," Willis admitted later when asked about the shirt. "I'm glad he didn't ask for it back."

This match was the equivalent of the All Blacks taking on Guam in the Rugby World Cup or Manchester United facing Barton Town Old Boys in the FA Cup. In sport, nevertheless, nothing is impossible. Had Iceland (population: 330,000) not just beaten England (population: 53 million) in football's European Championship?

If the rain which cut a swathe through the programme reflected the mood of a country in turmoil after the previous week's European referendum, this was an occasion to lift the spirits. Willis' extraordinary story had captured the public's imagination and the atmosphere under the Centre Court roof was joyful and raucous, with 15,000 fans cheering every winning point by the Warwick Boat Club coach. Willis, who was smiling from the moment he walked out, celebrated winners with gusto, raised his arms aloft after making successful Hawk-Eye challenges and stood with his arms outstretched in acknowledgement of the crowd's thunderous applause when he finally won a game, at the eighth attempt. Willis' family, friends and colleagues in his player box were regularly on their feet while his supporters' favourite song – 'Willbomb's on Fire' – rang around the stadium.

Federer won 6-0, 6-3, 6-4, but there were plenty of moments when Willis belied his lowly ranking. By the end the British No.23 was serving confidently, his final total of nine aces equalling Federer's. On occasions he outsmarted the Swiss with his clever drop shots and stop volleys, and he hit the shot of the match when a delightful lob ended a thrilling rally in the first set. Willis, who left The Championships with prize money of £50,000, said afterwards: "It was incredible. It was all just a blur. It was amazing. I did enjoy myself even though I was getting duffed up. I loved every bit of it. Not the duffing bit. I loved getting stuck in, fighting hard."

Willis, who described himself as having been an overweight "loser" in the past, agreed it had not been "my standard Wednesday" and said he would take away many happy memories. "I played a good point where I lobbed him," he said. "I can say I lobbed Roger Federer." The experience made him want to carry on working hard. "I think I have time to hit my peak in a few years," he said. "This is where I want to play tennis. I'm good enough. I have a lot to work on, a lot to improve."

After winning his first game Willis soaked up the acclaim from the crowd

Federer, who had only ever met one lower-ranked opponent in Grand Slam competition (he beat Devin Britton, the world No.1,370, at the 2009 US Open), joked afterwards that the last time he had enjoyed such little support at The Championships had been when he lost to Jiri Novak on his debut in 1999. However, he said that Willis had deserved the crowd's backing. "He played some great points," Federer said. "He fought hard. He has a great personality for a Centre Court [occasion] like this. It wasn't easy for him just to come out there and play a decent match. There was a lot of pressure on him as well. I thought he handled it great."

He added: "I'll remember most of my Centre Court matches here at Wimbledon, but this one will stand out because it's that special and probably not going to happen again for me to play against a guy 770 in the world. That's what stands out the most for me – the support he got, the great points he played."

Those who played under the Centre Court roof were the lucky ones on a day of prolonged rain interruptions. In the opening match Agnieszka Radwanska extended her 100 per cent record in the first round at The Championships when she beat Ukraine's Kateryna Kozlova 6-2, 6-1, after which the No.3 seed planned an afternoon in front of the television. "Now there are two good matches, Novak and Roger, so I have plenty of tennis to watch," she said.

Novak Djokovic was next on Centre Court and wasted no time making another entry in the history books as he beat France's Adrian Mannarino 6-4, 6-3, 7-6(5) despite eight double faults, including one which cost him the game when he served for the match at 5-4. It was Djokovic's 30th victory in succession at Grand Slam tournaments, which set a record for the Open era, beating Rod Laver's mark of 29, which the Australian set in 1969 and 1970. Djokovic's last defeat had been against Stan Wawrinka in the French Open final in 2015.

With Federer becoming the third straight-sets winner in a row on Centre Court, there was time for two more matches to be switched under the roof. Belinda Bencic beat Tsvetana Pironkova 6-2, 6-3 before Eugenie Bouchard completed a 6-3, 6-4 victory over Magdalena Rybarikova in a match which had begun 24 hours earlier on Court 12 before play was called off for the day early in the second set. Having waited all day for the chance to resume, Bouchard had been expecting to have to finish the match on Thursday until the late summons to Centre Court, where she had not played since losing to Petra Kvitova in the 2014 final.

"I was on the same couch for about six hours straight," the Canadian said of her time waiting in the locker room. "It was a very, very challenging day. It's obviously the same for both players and a lot of the players today. It's what I guess you have to expect a little bit. You have to embrace it and see it as not something so negative because you are at Wimbledon. But it's so challenging to know when to eat and try and nap. You keep yourself half-awake because it's raining. It's that on-off situation all day so it's tough."

Bouchard's reward was a second-round meeting with Britain's Johanna Konta, who also needed two days to complete her opening victory. Leading Monica Puig 2-1 in

Brolly bad show

Exactly one year since we were ducking for cover under umbrellas to protect ourselves from the hottest temperatures ever recorded at Wimbledon, the brollies were up again. Only this time, sadly, it was just wet, wet, wet...

Prolonged showers savaged the Wednesday Order of Play, with 40 singles matches either postponed entirely or suspended while in progress and only 18 of the billed 74 matches being completed.

The only consolation was that, for the first time since the middle Saturday of 2007, the All England Club offered a rain refund to spectators – a full refund for No.1 Court ticket holders and a partial refund for Grounds Pass ticket holders.

the second set when the match resumed, Konta went on to claim her first win at The Championships at the fifth attempt, winning 6-1, 7-5. "I'm very happy with my performance," Konta said after recovering from 4-2 down in the second set. Since The Championships 2015 Konta has enjoyed a richly successful 12 months, highlighted by her run to the semi-finals of the Australian Open. Having been ranked No.126 in the world at last year's Wimbledon, she began this year's tournament at No.19 and was the first British woman to be seeded since Jo Durie in 1984.

Kvitova had arrived at The Championships in modest form, having won only two matches in her first two tournaments on grass, but the 2011 and 2014 champion won her opening match with plenty to spare, crushing Sorana Cirstea 6-0, 6-4. "I think for fans it was a little bit cold," Kvitova said afterwards, before adding with a smile: "I made it quick, so that's good."

Dominic Thiem and Alexander Zverev, two of the game's most exciting young talents, were also quick off the mark as both beat experienced opponents in little more than an hour and a half. Thiem beat Florian Mayer 7-5, 6-4, 6-4 to avenge his defeat by the German a fortnight earlier in the semi-finals at Halle, while Zverev beat Paul-Henri Mathieu 6-3, 6-4, 6-2.

Tomas Berdych and Bernard Tomic, seeded No.10 and No.19 respectively, completed victories after their matches had been suspended the previous evening. Berdych beat Ivan Dodig 7-6(5), 5-7, 6-1, 7-6(2), while Tomic returned for a final set shoot-out against Fernando Verdasco. Tomic won 4-6, 6-3, 6-3, 3-6, 6-4.

With the backlog of matches growing, the decision was taken by the Referee's Office to play all first-round matches in the Gentlemen's Doubles over the best of three sets rather than five.

Former champion Petra Kvitova was so worried that the watching fans would get chilly in the unseasonal conditions that she wrapped up her match against Sorana Cirstea with the loss of just four games

Behind every man...

Jennifer Bate (centre) enjoys boyfriend Marcus Willis' Centre Court heroics

CHAMPIONSHIPS
Day 3
NOTEBOOK

● **Suddenly cast as the most famous woman at Wimbledon**, dentist Jennifer Bate, the girlfriend of Marcus Willis, had almost as many cameras trained on her during her partner's dream encounter with Roger Federer on Centre Court as on the tennis action.

Inevitably, Marcus was asked if he now planned to marry the woman who was responsible for him being here in the first place after she'd persuaded him to keep his career going.

"I haven't thought, to be honest," he smiled. "These whole few weeks have been a bit of a blur... but I do like her quite a bit."

● **Novak Djokovic is used to receiving a bewildering variety of questions** at press conferences, but what he's not used to is having a journalist offering him a paean of praise after one of his routine victories. The world No.1 needed a double take after his second-round victory over Adrian Mannarino when someone in the interview room suddenly piped up with what was not so much a question as a declaration of awe: "I keep looking to find a weakness in your game, and I can't do it!"

The normally loquacious Djokovic seemed to be floored when he realised who was addressing him. "Mr. Bollettieri, wow!" he spluttered on realising it was Nick Bollettieri, the world's most celebrated tennis coach, who was there doubling as an online columnist for *The Independent*.

The love-in, rather than normal interrogation, continued as the American grandee called him a credit to the game and Djoko responded by saying: "I'm honoured to have your presence at the press conference. I'm overwhelmed."

The new water sculpture commissioned for The Championships 2016

● **By the middle of this first week**, the new Championships water sculpture, which had been officially unveiled by HRH The Duke of Kent, President of The All England Lawn Tennis Club, on the opening Monday of The Championships, was drawing plenty of admiring glances from crowds gathering around it close to Court 18.

The abstract sculpture, made of green patinated bronze and named "Alchemilla" after the plant which can be found in the beautiful flower beds around the Grounds, was created by William Pye. The internationally acclaimed British artist was asked to create an artwork that would symbolise and celebrate the setting of tennis in an English garden.

"Accuracy, precision and precariousness are all aspects of this work and they also characterise much of what we experience when playing and watching tennis," said Pye, who more than half a century ago studied at Wimbledon School of Art.

DAY 4

THURSDAY
30 JUNE

The sun came out after two days of bad weather, but while the rain stopped falling the seeds continued to tumble. On a day full of upsets, 18 seeded singles players went out, including the 2015 runner-up, Garbiñe Muguruza, Britain's Johanna Konta, the French Open semi-finalist Dominic Thiem and a trio of experienced campaigners in David Ferrer, Gilles Simon and Ivo Karlovic. For good measure Jean-Julien Rojer and Horia Tecau, the defending champions in the Gentlemen's Doubles, also lost.

Muguruza's 3-6, 2-6 defeat by Jana Cepelova, the world No.124, completed a rollercoaster 12 months for the world No.2. The Championships 2015 had been a big breakthrough for Muguruza, whose elegant game and winning smile had made her an instant hit with the Centre Court crowd as she reached her first Grand Slam singles final before losing to Serena Williams.

However, coping with her new-found fame did not prove easy and she made early departures from the subsequent US Open and the 2016 Australian Open. Her talent, though, was never in doubt and everything went right for her at the French Open, where she beat Williams to claim her first Grand Slam singles title.

Having scraped through her first match at The Championships against Camila Giorgi, Muguruza looked badly out of touch on No.1 Court against Cepelova, who had knocked out Simona Halep on the same stage 12 months earlier. The 23-year-old Slovakian loves the big occasion. "I like to play against the biggest stars, of course, against the champions," she said.

Muguruza admitted: "My energy was missing a little bit today. I already felt a bit tired yesterday. During and after the match today I felt empty and I started to feel sick. But she played great, with no fear."

The 22-year-old Spaniard said she had returned to competition too early following her triumph in Paris. "I'm going to learn that you really need to concentrate on how to recover, and don't reach a moment where your energy is too low, especially to play a Grand Slam and to face opponents who are good and want to beat you so much," she said. "You've got to be ready. You cannot go out there not at your best."

Turning to Konta, one of the most significant moments in her rise had been her victory over Muguruza at the 2015 US Open, which at three hours and 23 minutes was the longest women's match in the tournament's history. Konta was only the second British woman to reach the fourth round at Flushing Meadows since 1991 and did even better at the Australian Open, where she became the first British woman to make the semi-finals of a Grand Slam singles tournament for 33 years.

However, building on those successes has proved difficult. Konta lost in the first round of the French Open and might have hoped for a less challenging start at The Championships, where she was the first British woman to be seeded since 1984. Monica Puig, who had just reached the semi-finals at Eastbourne, was a tricky opponent in the first round and Konta then faced Eugenie Bouchard, the 2014 runner-up, who was rediscovering her form after a miserable 2015.

Bouchard hit the ground running, making only one unforced error in the first set, and despite Konta's fightback the Canadian went on to win 6-3, 1-6, 6-1. Konta had her chances but failed to convert break points in Bouchard's first two service games in the third set. "I think it's my best performance of 2016," Bouchard said afterwards. "I have been working very hard, and I know that matches like this with a good performance will come, that it's just a question of time."

Konta had expected Bouchard to be a tough opponent. "Although her ranking may have gone down over the past year, her level of tennis never went away," Konta said. "I think I've got a lot of good things to take away from that match and a lot of things I hope to implement in my development as a tennis player and as a person."

Below left: Garbiñe Muguruza felt she had not fully recovered from her exertions in winning the French Open as she lost to Jana Cepelova

Below: Johanna Konta fought hard but was ultimately defeated by a resurgent Eugenie Bouchard

Far right: Greek qualifier Maria Sakkari was in hair-raising action against Venus Williams, taking the former champion to three sets in a thrilling match on Court 18

The British No.1's post-match mood was better than that of Heather Watson, who was bitterly frustrated by her 6-3, 0-6, 10-12 first-round defeat to Germany's Annika Beck, which had first been scheduled two days earlier and eventually got under way on Wednesday before rain stopped play early in the third set. The British No.2 lost nine games in a row after winning the first set but still had her chances in the third, when she had three match points. Watson, who said it was one of the biggest disappointments of her career, smashed her racket into the turf in anger. Two days later she was fined $12,000 for unsportsmanlike conduct, which was the second largest fine in the history of The Championships.

"After a loss like this, I'm so angry with myself, I feel like I need to punish myself," Watson revealed. "It wasn't a good day. I just went on Twitter. There was plenty [of abuse]."

Eleven ladies' seeds went out on this remarkable day of upsets. Belinda Bencic retired with a wrist injury when trailing Julia Boserup early in the second set, while Samantha Stosur was beaten 4-6, 2-6 by Sabine Lisicki, the 2013 runner-up. There were also straight-sets defeats for Karolina Pliskova (to Misaki Doi), Sara Errani (to Alize Cornet), Kristina Mladenovic (to Aliaksandra Sasnovich) and Andrea Petkovic (to Elena Vesnina). Jelena Jankovic was beaten 6-4, 6-7(1), 6-8 by Marina Erakovic after more than two and a half hours and there were also three-set defeats for Elina Svitolina (to Yaroslava Shvedova) and Caroline Garcia (to Katerina Siniakova).

Agnieszka Radwanska, the No.3 seed, survived a scare against Ana Konjuh, who took a medical time-out after twisting her right ankle when she accidentally stepped on a ball at 7-7 in the deciding set. Radwanska went on to win 6-2, 4-6, 9-7. Venus Williams also struggled before beating the Greek qualifier, Maria Sakkari, 7-5, 4-6, 6-3.

Seeds were also scattered in the Gentlemen's Singles, with Thiem's 6-7(4), 6-7(5), 6-7(3) defeat to Jiri Vesely perhaps the biggest surprise given that the Austrian had recently broken into the world's top 10. Simon lost 3-6, 6-7(1), 6-4, 4-6 to Grigor Dimitrov, a semi-finalist in 2014, having complained bitterly to the umpire, John Blom, after rain fell on the court. "I don't want to play, when it's raining, on grass," he said. "If I play and I get injured I will sue you."

Below: Heather Watson was hugely frustrated by her defeat to Annika Beck, the British No.2 losing the third set 10-12 after failing to convert three match points

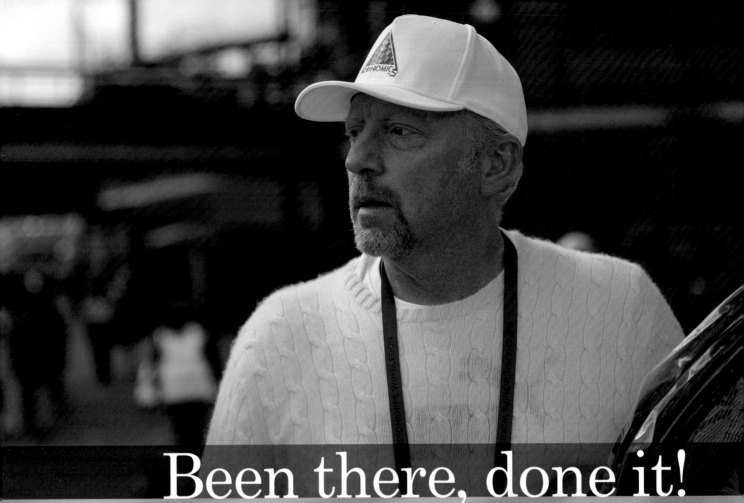

Been there, done it!

It's not just former men's Grand Slam winners and Wimbledon champions getting in on the act, as Martina Hingis (above) and Justine Henin were also working as mentors during Wimbledon 2016

They are the must-have accoutrements for every top player. Because though you may be good, it really helps if your coach was once just as good, and preferably rather better…

Indeed, the trend for 'super coaches', the men and women who have precious insights into the game that only come with being successful at a Grand Slam, had never seemed more popular than at this Wimbledon.

A cast of nine former men's and two former ladies' Grand Slam champions were on hand to help out the class of 2016.

Marin Cilic was being guided by his fellow Croat, 2001 champion Goran Ivanisevic, Richard Gasquet by double French Open champion Sergi Bruguera and Kei Nishikori by Michael Chang, who was famously victorious in the 1989 French

Open. Elsewhere, Stan Wawrinka was being mentored by 1996 Wimbledon champion Richard Krajicek while David Goffin found himself under the wing of 2002 Australian Open victor Thomas Johansson.

The seemingly unstoppable Novak Djokovic was still swearing by the help of three-time Wimbledon champion Boris Becker while Andy Murray had rejoined forces with his old mentor, Ivan Lendl, with immediate effect, having just picked up The Queen's Club title in their first week back together.

For coming man Milos Raonic, it wasn't good enough to just have former world No.1 Carlos Moya in his coaching team, so he also appointed John McEnroe to add a touch of fire to his own ice.

On the ladies' side, seven-time Grand Slam champion Justine Henin had been drafted in to help Ukrainian star Elina Svitolina while Martina Hingis, looking to defend her two doubles titles, was also seen in the box of her talented young Swiss compatriot Belinda Bencic.

So how is it that 'super coaches' can reach parts that other coaches can't? It is as Becker once said: "Champions know what it takes. It's not just about the tennis, it's about the mind."

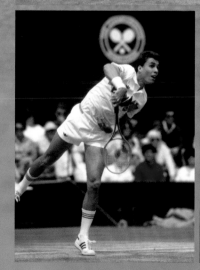

Past Grand Slam winners Ivan Lendl, John McEnroe and Boris Becker have added a new dimension to The Championships as coaches to Andy Murray, Milos Raonic and Novak Djokovic respectively

Elsewhere Ferrer was beaten by grass court specialist Nicolas Mahut, and Karlovic lost to Slovakia's Lukas Lacko. Viktor Troicki was beaten in five sets by Albert Ramos-Vinolas and Benoit Paire lost to John Millman.

Alexandr Dolgopolov, the No.30 seed, was beaten 6-7(6), 4-6, 1-6 by Dan Evans, the match having resumed after play had been called off the previous evening with the first set about to go into a tie-break. Evans hit the ball consistently throughout to earn a third-round meeting with Roger Federer.

The 26-year-old Briton, renowned for his cheeky sense of humour, was asked if he had had a chance to speak to his good friend, Marcus Willis, who had lost to Federer the previous day. "Are you kidding me?" Evans said. "You don't get a word out of him. He's a celebrity now. He just looks at his phone. I spoke to him yesterday and it was like speaking to a brick wall." Would he be seeking advice from Willis? "No. He lost in three straights. No advice needed." Evans also joked that he was surprised the All England Club had let Willis wear his shirt with the 'RF' logo. "It was slightly off-white," the world No.91 said with a smile. "I don't know how long he's had it. I've shared a room with him. It might not have even been clean."

Evans, whose rise in the rankings earlier in the year saw four British men ranked inside the world's top 100 for the first time since 1978, said that tennis in Britain was "definitely going upwards". He added: "I think this Wimbledon has opened the eyes to people that we're actually pretty good at tennis." Evans used to have a reputation as a party animal but said he had learned the need to work hard. "I still like a night out," he added. "I just do it at the right time."

Andy Murray continued his impressive progress with an emphatic 6-3, 6-2, 6-1 victory over Yen-Hsun Lu, who led 3-1 in the opening set but then lost 17 of the next 20 games. Lu went into the match unbeaten in his previous 11 matches on grass, having won two Challenger titles in the build-up to The Championships, but with Murray returning serve beautifully and hitting some delightful drop shots, the world No.76 was comprehensively outplayed. Murray, who enjoyed a royal audience with Camilla, Duchess of Cornwall after coming off court, said: "I was obviously creating a lot of chances in the second and third sets. It wasn't easy for him to win games. I wasn't giving up any mistakes on return and I was dictating a lot of the points. I used quite a lot of variety. I used the slice a lot and changes of pace. It was good."

The first surprise of the Gentlemen's Doubles came with the opening-round defeat of the defending champions, Rojer and Tecau, who went down 2-6, 6-7(3) to Canada's Adil Shamasdin and his British partner, Jonny Marray, who won the title with Freddie Nielsen in 2012.

Grigor Dimitrov takes a time-out during his feisty four-set victory over Gilles Simon

Victor joins the club

With his tantrum on Court 17, Viktor Troicki was following in the footsteps of legends

CHAMPIONSHIPS Day 4 NOTEBOOK

• **Every now and again Wimbledon witnesses a player in glorious meltdown.** Down the years, players like John McEnroe ("You cannot be serious!"), Jeff Tarango ("Oh, shut up!") and Ilie Nastase ("Call me Mr Nastase") have gone off like exploding fireworks during matches.

So, welcome to the exclusive club, Viktor Troicki.

The Serbian No.25 seed added his name to the 'infamy, infamy, they've all got it in for me' brigade in the dying embers of his second-round match with Albert Ramos-Vinolas on Court 17.

With the Spaniard serving for the match at 5-3, 30-30 in the fifth set, his first serve was called out, until Italian umpire Damiano Torella overruled, leaving Troicki match point down.

Cue the explosion. "No way, look at it," Troicki shouted at Torella, showing him that the ball had no chalk on it so could not possibly have hit the line. "You're the worst umpire ever in the world! What are you doing? Did you see the ball? You're so bad!"

After earning a warning for unsportsmanlike conduct, he lost the match on the next point and then resumed his diatribe. His departing shot before marching off to the Referee's Office was: "You're horrible!" Surely another phrase to enter Wimbledon's hall of famous abuse.

• **Everyone loved Bud Collins**, the larger-than-life *Boston Globe* reporter and American TV broadcaster who, after more than half a century in the game, became one of tennis' most colourful and irrepressible personalities and who, clad in those glorious strawberry trousers, always seemed to shine most brightly at Wimbledon.

Sadly, he died in March 2016, aged 86, but to ensure that generations in the future would always be able to smile about Bud's unique sartorial style and his overriding sense of fun, Collins' widow Anita Ruthling Klaussen came to the club to donate one of his most special, garish outfits to the Wimbledon Lawn Tennis Museum.

"This outfit was very special. Bud would only wear it for the Gentlemen's Singles Final at Wimbledon," Anita explained, after handing over a black blazer, pink gingham shirt, red-and-polka-dotted bow tie, leather shoes, red-and-black striped socks plus, of course, those wonderful trousers that lit up the All England Club just like the man himself did.

• **Gone but not forgotten**, news reached the Grounds that Marcus Willis had turned out, just 24 hours after his match with Roger Federer on Centre Court, at the less celebrated venue of Coventry and North Warwickshire Tennis Club to play a Coventry League doubles match for his Warwick Boat Club team. In keeping with the fairytale, Willis won his match with doubles partner Gavin Henderson, explaining to his clubmates that playing Federer had "just been a warm-up" for the big one in Coventry.

DAY
5

FRIDAY
1 JULY

As the rain returned with a vengeance after Thursday's brief respite, there was at least one person grateful for the downpour on Day 5 that finally brought an early end to play everywhere other than on Centre Court. Novak Djokovic, the defending Gentlemen's Singles champion, was in dire straits on No.1 Court when the weather came to his rescue.

After another day punctuated by frustrating rain delays, Djokovic and Sam Querrey had had to wait until just before 7pm to walk out on court. When rain sent them scurrying back to the locker room less than 90 minutes later, Djokovic was trailing 6-7(6), 1-6. Play was soon abandoned for the day, earning the Serb a desperately needed reprieve.

Djokovic won only four points against Querrey's booming serve before the 28-year-old American took the opening set on a tie-break. As the champion looked increasingly out of sorts, Querrey won the second set in just 22 minutes. Comparisons were being made that evening with Djokovic's experience at The Championships 2015, when he had recovered from two sets down to beat Kevin Anderson in a fourth-round match spread over two days. On that occasion, however, Djokovic had already levelled the contest at two sets apiece when play was called off for the day. This time he would have to come out the next afternoon and win three sets in a row to stay alive.

It was a day to be grateful if you were playing under the Centre Court roof, although that was probably not the feeling uppermost in Stan Wawrinka's mind as the No.4 seed became the most significant scalp so far in the Gentlemen's Singles when he was beaten 6-3, 3-6, 6-7(2), 3-6 by Juan Martin del Potro. Wawrinka is a popular figure, but there could be no mistaking the crowd's excitement at witnessing such a memorable victory for Del Potro. The 6ft 6in Argentinian, a gentle giant, admitted afterwards that his hands were shaking in a rare moment of joy after seven years dogged by wrist problems. "The crowd was unbelievable with me," he said. "The atmosphere was amazing."

Since winning the 2009 US Open, Del Potro has undergone three wrist operations, after each of which he endured lengthy rehabilitation. Having returned in February after an 11-month break, he was appearing in his first Grand Slam tournament for two and a half years and his first Wimbledon since 2013, when he had lost to Djokovic in a memorable five-set semi-final. The meeting with Wawrinka was the first time two Grand Slam champions had met in the second round at The Championships since Marat Safin beat Djokovic in 2008.

Del Potro's continuing problems with his wrist were evident in the way he rarely hit his formidable two-handed backhand, choosing for the most part to play one-handed slices instead. His forehand, nevertheless, remained a huge weapon and he proved he had lost none of his mental strength when he fought back after losing the first set. "My backhand is not 100 per cent yet, because now I'm playing too many slices," he said afterwards. "I know how far I am from my highest level. I've been working hard to be 100 per cent for next season.

"It was really tough to come back to the sport after my third operation, but now I'm enjoying tennis again," he added. "I don't know if I can be in the top positions again, but if not I will be happy just to be playing tennis."

Wawrinka meanwhile was left to reflect on the fact that Wimbledon is the only Grand Slam tournament where he has failed to reach the semi-finals. However, he said he was pleased for Del Potro. "For sure we are all happy that he's back. He's a great guy off the court. He's an amazing player on the court. He's a big champion."

Remembering the fallen

At 07.28 on Friday morning, amid the pouring rain, the Wimbledon Grounds came to a standstill to observe a two-minute silence, a sombre and dignified tribute to the thousands of soldiers who were killed at the Battle of the Somme in the First World War, which started at precisely this time exactly 100 years ago to the day.

Later in the day it was the turn of another Swiss to walk on to Centre Court. Forty-eight hours after beating Marcus Willis, Roger Federer faced another home player in Dan Evans. Twelve months previously Evans had been ranked No.763 in the world – just nine places ahead of where his good friend Willis currently sat – but after a year of hard work the 26-year-old from Birmingham had broken into the top 100 for the first time. Having recorded his first victory at the All England Club by beating Jan-Lennard Struff in the first round, the world No.91 then knocked out Alexandr Dolgopolov, the No.30 seed, in the second.

Evans, who had never played Federer before or competed on Centre Court, had his moments, but ended up being handed a "drumming", to use his own description, as the seven-times champion won 6-4, 6-2, 6-2. With Evans struggling to hold serve, Federer made flying starts to each set. He led 4-0 in both the first and second sets and was 5-1 up in the third before Evans held to love when serving to stay in the match.

Saying he would treasure every memory of the match, Evans admitted afterwards that it had been "surreal" to see Federer on the other side of the net. "It was tough to get used to," he said. "There were so many people. It was very different to what I am used to. I didn't expect it to be so sort of on top of me. It was just an amazing experience just to play him."

He added: "Obviously everyone dreams about playing Federer on Centre Court. Two Brits got a chance this year. That should be inspiration for a lot of people. It's inspiration for me that I got a chance to play him. I want that again, to play other good players on those courts."

Earlier in the day No.2 Court had been the place to be as Nick Kyrgios beat Dustin Brown 6-7(3), 6-1, 2-6, 6-4, 6-4 in a see-saw contest between two big crowd-pleasers. In a quickfire contest that barely lasted two hours, a total of 133 winners were struck, including a wonderful through-the-legs drop-shot winner by Brown. Acknowledging his opponent's brilliant shot-making, Kyrgios said afterwards: "There were times out there where you literally don't want to play. You just want to put the racket down. That's what you get from him. He's going to hit jumping backhands that are going to hit the fence, but then he's going to hit three of the greatest volleys that you've ever seen."

The contest between the flamboyant Dustin Brown **(left)** and the maverick talent of Nick Kyrgios was one match everyone wanted to see

Previous pages: During the late afternoon of Day 5, the sun finally broke through and at last the Grounds were bathed in that glorious summer light that make an evening of tennis down at London SW19 one of the delights of the English summer

Serena and Venus Williams both won but only after being taken to deciding sets. Serena said she had needed to go into "warrior mode" to beat her fellow American, Christina McHale, 6-7(7), 6-2, 6-4, while Venus survived the challenge of Russia's Daria Kasatkina to win 7-5, 4-6, 10-8.

At 5-4 and 40-30 Serena thought she had won the first set when a McHale forehand was called long. The world No.1 was walking back to her chair when Hawk-Eye showed that the ball had caught the baseline. The defending champion's anger at losing the subsequent tie-break was evident as she thumped her racket into the ground at a changeover before throwing it, inadvertently, into the lap of a cameraman sitting behind her, an incident which cost her a fine of $10,000 the following day. "I was just really, really, really angry," she said later. "I had a lot of chances."

Williams restored order in the second set but had to come from behind in the third after McHale went 2-0 up. "It's very difficult to break me down mentally," Williams said. "I think I'm amazing when it comes to tight matches and getting through it, just really fighting till the end. I don't give up."

Asked about the smashed racket, which she gave away to a fan after the match, Williams said: "I've cracked a number of rackets throughout my career. I've been fined a number of times for cracking rackets. In fact, I look at it like I didn't crack one at the French Open or Rome, so I was doing really good."

Christina McHale (below) gave Serena Williams her toughest test yet, the defending champion requiring all her resources of power and resilience to eventually triumph in three sets while sister Venus eventually triumphed 10-8 in the final set of an epic, rain-interrupted contest against the brilliant Russian teenager Daria Kasatkina (below right)

Kasatkina was born less than two months before 36-year-old Venus Williams played her first match at The Championships in 1997. The 19-year-old Russian made the biggest rankings jump since last year of all seeded singles players at this year's tournament, having climbed 128 places to No.33. At 7-6 in the deciding set play was stopped on match point to Williams as rain interrupted proceedings for a third time. When they returned Kasatkina saved the match point, but Williams went on to secure her victory after two hours and 41 minutes.

British interest in the Ladies' Singles ended when Svetlana Kuznetsova beat Tara Moore 6-1, 2-6, 6-3. Moore, who enjoyed her best grass court season, had never won a match at The Championships until this year, but the 23-year-old Briton gave Kuznetsova some anxious moments. The momentum was with Moore after the world No.227 claimed the second set, but Kuznetsova took a hold on the decider with an early break. Moore, who was thrilled by the loud support on No.3 Court, said afterwards: "I tried my best. I threw my house at her and ultimately came back with nothing."

Manuel's golden Wimbledon memories

The great Manuel Santana (above left) and legendary coach Nick Bollettieri appeared to be enjoying The Championships immensely

● **Exactly 50 years to the day when he beat American Dennis Ralston** 6-4, 11-9, 6-4 to become the first man from his country ever to win the Wimbledon title, Manuel Santana returned to Centre Court.

Now 78 and still active in the game as director of the Madrid Open, 'Manolo', wearing the gold watch he received for his 1966 victory, gave a wistful smile as he celebrated the golden jubilee of his triumph. He had once famously said grass was "only for cows" until he learned to fall in love with Wimbledon and blazed a trail for 10 future Spanish Grand Slam champions, both men and women.

His prize, he remembered, was a voucher worth less than £20 that he had to spend on tennis gear at Lillywhites sports shop, and as there were no courtesy cars for players in those days and he couldn't afford a taxi, he often took the tube, got off at Southfields and walked up to the All England Club with his bag and three rackets.

● **It was as if John Isner was being taunted.** Each time his second-round match on Court 18 against Matthew Barton was interrupted for a rain stoppage, he would have to walk past the plaque that commemorates his now legendary win over Nicolas Mahut in 2010, the longest tennis match ever played.

"It's hard not to feel emotional, especially when that plaque is sitting there," said the big American after his successful return to the court which provided the stage for one of Wimbledon's most celebrated stories.

"You hear people in the crowd saying, 'Oh, this is your court.' But on the way there today, walking up to it, I didn't look at that plaque at all. I wanted to block it out and try not to think too much about that match."

He did just that, going on to win 7-6(8), 7-6(3), 7-6(8), and was immensely grateful that no 70-68 final set was required this time!

Play is suspended on No. 1 Court with Venus Williams on match point

● **Venus Williams felt like she was in a movie** as her match with the brilliant Russian teenager Daria Kasatkina was interrupted by rain just as she held a match point at 7-6 in the final set, something she had never experienced in her two decades at the top.

When they resumed, Kasatkina saved the point and fought on until Williams finally emerged victorious at 10-8. "The interruption at match point was probably not ideal," Venus smiled. "She handled it well. She played smart. It was just non-stop action. It was like a Hollywood script!"

DAY
6
SATURDAY
2 JULY

I t says everything about Novak Djokovic's remarkable powers of recovery that he was still viewed by many as the favourite to beat Sam Querrey when their third-round match resumed on No.1 Court. Never mind that the big-serving American had won the first two sets the previous evening or that Djokovic had looked decidedly out-of-sorts before rain halted play for the day.

This was a man who had won the last two Wimbledons, reached the final of eight of his last nine Grand Slam tournaments, topped the world rankings for the last two years and repeatedly dug himself out of tricky situations like this. Surely nerves would have got to Querrey overnight as he contemplated the enormity of what he could achieve, while Djokovic would recover the strength and composure he had seemed to lack in the 72 minutes they had spent on court.

For a while that was exactly how the match seemed to be working out. On the resumption Djokovic won the first five games, faltered momentarily when Querrey retrieved one break but then served out to take the third set. The world No.1 still looked a little below his best, but seemed to be turning the match around despite Querrey's thunderous serves and forehands.

Querrey hung on in the fourth set, saving 11 out of 12 break points. At 4-4, however, Djokovic converted his fourth break point of the game with a forehand winner to give himself the chance to serve out and level the match. Querrey, nevertheless, broke back for 5-5 and the set went to a tie-break. Even then Djokovic had the upper hand at the start, but after leading 3-1 he lost five of the next six points. At 4-6 down the

Serb saved the first match point with an ace, but a stray forehand on the second handed Querrey the biggest victory of his career. In winning 7-6(6), 6-1, 3-6, 7-6(5), Querrey had pounded down 31 aces and hit 56 winners, which was 22 more than his opponent had managed.

Djokovic's defeat ended some remarkable sequences, including the world No.1's 28 consecutive appearances in quarter-finals at Grand Slam events, his run of 16 successive match victories at The Championships and his Open era record of 30 consecutive Grand Slam match wins. The defeat also ended the three-times Wimbledon champion's attempt to become only the second man, after Don Budge, to win five Grand Slam titles in a row.

After his earliest loss at The Championships for seven years, there was inevitably speculation as to Djokovic's physical and mental well-being. Was he simply drained emotionally after being at the top of the game for so long? Was the fact that his average serving speeds were down – 112mph on first serve and 93mph on second – an indication that he had a shoulder problem? Had he been injured in a fall during his second-round match? Djokovic did not want to discuss his physical condition but said he would not be playing in Serbia's forthcoming Davis Cup quarter-final against Britain and declined to say where he would compete next. When asked if he was 100 per cent fit, he replied: "Not really, but this is not the place and time to talk about it."

Instead Djokovic paid tribute to Querrey: "He played a terrific match. He served very well, as he usually does. I think that part of his game was brutal today. He made a lot of free points with the first serve. He just overpowered me."

Djokovic did not think he had been burdened by the weight of history. "I believe in positive things in life," he said. "I managed to win four Grand Slams in a row. I want to try to focus on that rather than on failure." He added: "It's not the first time that I've lost a Grand Slam match, or any match for that matter. I know what to do. First things first: just to put my mind at ease and relax. I'll think about something different."

Querrey admitted that he had not gone into the match thinking he would win. "He's played at such a high level for so long," the world No.41 said. "What makes him so good is that he wins those matches where he isn't playing his best. In the second set yesterday he definitely lost some momentum. He wasn't playing like he usually does.

"Today he made me earn it. He's not a guy that goes away. He made me come out and win those big points. It was probably not the best he's ever played, but not the worst either."

News of Djokovic's defeat did not take long to reach the man who would be the most likely to benefit. Andy Murray, the world No.2, was in the second set of his third-round match against Australia's John Millman when Djokovic's result was flashed up on the Centre Court scoreboard, to gasps from the crowd. Murray admitted after his 6-3, 7-5, 6-2 victory over the world No.67 that he could not help noticing the news. "Obviously if you see a result or hear the fans, then you think about it," he said. "You don't just not see what's going on and you think about it. But it wasn't something that was going through my mind for more than 10 or 15 seconds."

Murray said Djokovic's defeat would not affect his own thinking for the rest of the competition. "If I was to reach the final, then it may have some bearing, but it doesn't right now," he said. "My draw's still exactly the same."

He added: "Rather than it being a surprise, what Novak's actually done should really be almost celebrated now. It's incredible. He broke a number of records, winning all four Slams and 30 consecutive Grand Slam matches. It's amazing. Obviously I would imagine today he'd be disappointed, but, looking back, it's been probably the best 12 months in tennis for years."

Murray had needed to remain focused on his own task after two rain breaks, the first of them at the start of the second set. When the players returned it started raining again after only two more points, upon

Russia's Ekaterina Makarova defeated Petra Kvitova, in the last match to be completed in the second round

A day to remember

Middle Saturday at Wimbledon once again had a soaring feel as Centre Court enjoyed honouring the heroic members of our Armed Forces and also some of the country's top sports personalities in the Royal Box.

Nicola Adams, the first woman to win an Olympic boxing gold medal, record-breaking England cricketers Jimmy Anderson and Stuart Broad, and Britain's six-time Olympic gold medallist, cyclist Sir Chris Hoy were among the sporting luminaries.

In the month that marked the golden jubilee of English football's finest hour, the World Cup victory, there was a special roar for some of the boys of '66 – Gordon Banks, Sir Bobby Charlton, Sir Geoff Hurst, Roger Hunt and Ron Flowers, along with Stephanie Moore, representing her late husband and team captain, the great Bobby Moore.

Another treat was being able to see the Davis Cup, the World Cup of men's team tennis, being paraded by the squad who, in 2015, won the trophy for Great Britain for the first time since 1936.

Captain Leon Smith, James Ward, Jamie Murray, Dan Evans and Kyle Edmund took a lap of honour, with only Dom Inglot and Andy Murray missing out on the celebration, the latter as he was preparing for his third-round match against John Millman.

Yet the crowd saved their biggest salute for 93-year-old Joy Lofthouse (*left*), who had been a Spitfire pilot during the Second World War and, just the year before, had flown one of the famous planes again at the age of 92! The Centre Court recognised a truly special lady with an ovation from the heart.

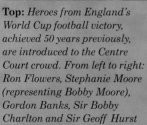

Top: *Heroes from England's World Cup football victory, achieved 50 years previously, are introduced to the Centre Court crowd. From left to right: Ron Flowers, Stephanie Moore (representing Bobby Moore), Gordon Banks, Sir Bobby Charlton and Sir Geoff Hurst*

Above: *Clockwise left to right: David Beckham (football), Brian O'Driscoll (rugby), Nicola Adams (boxing), Sir Chris Hoy (cycling), Jimmy Anderson (cricket) and the ever-popular Billie Jean King*

Right: *Great Britain Davis Cup captain Leon Smith (left) and members of the squad parade the Davis Cup*

which the roof was closed for the rest of the match. In completing his third successive straight-sets victory Murray reached the second week of his 22nd Grand Slam tournament in succession, while his 49th victory at The Championships took him one clear of his coach Ivan Lendl's career total.

Querrey's doubles partner, Steve Johnson, also reached the last 16, beating Grigor Dimitrov 6-7(6), 7-6(3), 6-4, 6-2, while Nicolas Mahut beat his own doubles partner, Pierre-Hugues Herbert, 7-6(5), 6-4, 3-6, 6-3. Alexander Zverev, aged 19, beat 34-year-old Mikhail Youzhny 6-4, 3-6, 6-0, 4-6, 6-2, while Milos Raonic claimed his third successive straight-sets victory, beating Jack Sock 7-6(2), 6-4, 7-6(1).

Above: Simona Halep overcame an Achilles injury to beat Kiki Bertens

Petra Kvitova, the Ladies' Singles champion of 2011 and 2014, failed to reach the second week of a Grand Slam event for the third time this year when she was beaten 5-7, 6-7(5) by Russia's Ekaterina Makarova in the last second-round match to be completed. "I felt stuck in the second round for a while," the Czech said afterwards. "I was waiting all day long almost every day to be scheduled on, and didn't really have a chance to finish or step on the court."

Kvitova said she needed "stability and peace" in the wake of an exhausting first six months of the year. Having split from her long-time coach, David Kotyza, Kvitova said she was still adjusting to working alongside his replacement, Frantisek Cermak. "Hopefully everything will get better and be more settled for me," she said. "I have got a brilliant team around me."

Eugenie Bouchard, who lost to Kvitova in the 2014 final, was beaten 4-6, 3-6 by Dominika Cibulkova. The Canadian thumped her racket into the court in frustration and admitted afterwards: "I was definitely a bit emotional out there. It's frustrating to feel like you're not playing your best tennis at Wimbledon."

Simona Halep, who had not played any warm-up tournaments on grass because of an Achilles problem, eased to a 6-4, 6-3 victory over Kiki Bertens. "For three days I had unbelievable pain," Halep said of her injury. "I couldn't walk, and then it was gone. Then after a few days here I started to feel it again, but the next day it went."

Jana Cepelova, who knocked out the 2015 runner-up Garbiñe Muguruza in the second round, lost 6-4, 1-6, 10-12 to Lucie Safarova, while the Australian Open champion, Angelique Kerber, beat her fellow German, Carina Witthoeft, 7-6(11), 6-1.

Lleyton Hewitt, who previously retired from professional tennis after the Australian Open at the beginning of the year, took a wild card into the Gentlemen's Doubles alongside Jordan Thompson. The Australians saved eight match points before beating Nicolas Almagro and David Marrero 6-7(6), 6-4, 19-17 after nearly four hours. The third set alone took nearly two and a half hours.

Given the continuing weather delays it was just as well that the All England Club had announced on Friday evening that there would be play on Middle Sunday for only the fourth time in the tournament's 139-year history and for the first time since 2004. At 1pm on Saturday it was announced that tickets would go on sale online at 3pm. All 22,000 were accounted for in just 27 minutes.

The royal box rocks

Hands up if you're having fun!

● **Perhaps getting themselves in the mood for Middle Sunday**, when Mexican waves around Centre Court have always been popular, it was a delight to see English football icon David Beckham and his mum Sandra rising to their feet, along with the All England Club chairman Philip Brook, to ensure the Royal Box did not miss out on the fun.

● **What a rare treat it was to see the Davis Cup** being paraded around Centre Court on a lap of honour by the first British team for 79 years (minus Dom Inglot and Andy Murray, who was otherwise engaged preparing for his third-round match) to win one of the sport's most hallowed prizes last year.

Even more marvellous, although the crowd didn't even realise, was that this was not the replica trophy that is normally used on such occasions but the real thing, the original sterling silver Davis Cup punchbowl that dates back 116 years.

The replica trophy was still in transit on Saturday morning so a hasty decision was made to request the use of the original Cup on a rare excursion from its Roehampton home, where it is kept under lock and key at the International Tennis Federation headquarters.

● **The kiosk near Court 14** was doing its usual roaring trade in used match balls but this was a particularly special year to snap up one of the 50,000-plus Slazengers that featured at The Championships, as this year marked the 30th anniversary of the yellow balls being used at Wimbledon for the first time.

The International Tennis Federation had actually introduced the

Great Britain captain Leon Smith parades the actual Davis Cup on Centre Court

yellow ball in 1972 as research had shown them to be more visible to TV viewers but Wimbledon, still using white balls that tended to rapidly take on a greenish hue, a characteristic which made life difficult for the players, took another 14 years before succumbing to their charms.

● **Feliciano Lopez, locked in fascinating** but unfinished third-round combat with Nick Kyrgios on No.1 Court, is still going strong at 34 but when the Spaniard calls it a day, perhaps he will have another sporting string to his bow.

For Sam Querrey explained that, to while away the hours, the players had taken to having putting competitions on a makeshift green set up in the locker room. "I didn't see it, but I heard Lopez made 14 in a row the other day," he said, sounding mightily impressed.

MIDDLE
SUNDAY

SUNDAY
3 JULY

Tomas Berdych thought it was "very special" but John Isner said it felt no different to any other day. Coco Vandeweghe said it was "amazing" and "quite cool" while Richard Gasquet had a "strange feeling" about it. Nick Kyrgios said it was "really good" but Serena Williams "thought it would feel really different but it didn't".

Previous pages: The enthralled Middle Sunday crowd were served up a treat on No.2 Court with the conclusion of an epic five-setter between Jo-Wilfried Tsonga and marathon match specialist John Isner, with Tsonga finally triumphing 19-17 in the final set

There were plenty of contrasting opinions about Middle Sunday, but the one certainty was that the decision to add the extra day's play had put The Championships back on track after a first week punctuated by frequent stoppages of rain. Playing matches on Middle Sunday, when there was a marked improvement in the weather, ensured that the Gentlemen's and Ladies' Singles would be up to speed. By the end of play the third round had been completed in both events, which meant that all 16 fourth-round singles matches could be scheduled for the following day as originally planned.

It was only the fourth occasion in the history of The Championships and the first time for 12 years that matches were played on Middle Sunday. Having learned from past experience in dealing with the crowds on what is normally a rest day, the All England Club had made available only 22,000 tickets, which was little more than half the average attendance during the first week. Many more could have been sold – more than 110,000 people went online to try to buy them as the tickets sold out in just 27 minutes the previous day – but restricting the numbers ensured a comfortable and enjoyable experience for everyone who attended. A total of 10,000 tickets were sold for Centre Court and 8,000 for No.1 Court, with another 4,000 sold as Grounds Passes. It meant there were few queues and ensured good access to the outside courts in particular.

Play on all courts began at 11.30am and Coco Vandeweghe relished the opportunity to be first out on Centre Court. "It was really quite exciting," the American said after her 6-3, 6-4 victory over Roberta Vinci, the No.6 seed. "When I walked out, the roar of the crowd was, like, crazy. It was super loud. It made me giggle a little bit because it was just surprising."

Even before the match started Mexican waves were sweeping around the stadium. The atmosphere inspired Vandeweghe, who had been a quarter-finalist 12 months earlier. The No.27 seed made the most of her 6ft 1in frame to outmuscle Vinci, who had thwarted Serena Williams' attempt to win a calendar-year Grand Slam in the semi-finals of the previous year's US Open.

Williams was next up on Centre Court. After the stunning defeat of Novak Djokovic, the men's world No.1, 24 hours earlier, might his female counterpart suffer the same fate? Not a chance. There was not even a hint of the fragility Williams had shown against Christina McHale in the previous round as she crushed Germany's Annika Beck 6-3, 6-0 in just 51 minutes, winning 24 of the last 28 points. It was the 34-year-old American's 300th victory at a Grand Slam tournament, which took her clear of Chris Evert (299 wins) and left her second on the Open era list behind Martina Navratilova (306 wins).

Williams said she could understand the weight of expectation on Djokovic's shoulders. "Every time I step out on the court, if I don't win, it's major national news," she said. "But if I do win, it's just like a small tag in the corner." She drew parallels between her own achievements and Djokovic's. "I think he and I have both made extreme history," she said. "He's won four [Grand Slam titles] in a row. I won four in a row last year."

Far left: All the tickets for only the fourth Middle Sunday ever were snapped up in under half an hour

Below: First up on Centre Court, Coco Vandeweghe relished the "exciting" atmosphere as she powered past Roberta Vinci

A special atmosphere

It happens rarely so when Wimbledon opened its doors for just the fourth time in 130 editions on Middle Sunday, it really was a day to be savoured. A quarter-of-a-century since the original, chaotic 'People's Sunday', things may have been a bit calmer this year but the tennis was dramatic, the sun was out, the fun was spontaneous, and it was another of those great Wimbledon occasions to be able to boast, "I was there..."

The win over Beck earned Williams a fourth-round meeting with a familiar rival, Svetlana Kuznetsova, who beat Sloane Stephens 6-7(1), 6-2, 8-6 to reach the last 16 for the first time since 2008. The 31-year-old Russian won despite being given a code violation for on-court coaching by the umpire, Marijana Veljovic, who said Carlos Martinez had been coaching her from the sidelines. An unhappy Kuznetsova shouted at Veljovic: "I bet you all my prize money he didn't say anything." The incident seemed to disrupt Kuznetsova's rhythm, but after going 5-2 down in the deciding set she recovered to win six of the next seven games and take the match.

Jo-Wilfried Tsonga and John Isner also went the distance in a marathon contest that lasted four hours and 24 minutes. The match had been suspended the previous evening because of bad light after three sets. Isner, who famously beat Nicolas Mahut over 11 hours at The Championships in 2010 in the longest recorded match in history, failed to convert a match point at 15-16 in the deciding set and Tsonga went on to win 6-7(3), 3-6, 7-6(5), 6-2, 19-17. "I was a little tired," Isner admitted afterwards. "I knew the match could go a long way, but I wasn't thinking about what happened six years ago."

Juan Martin del Potro's first return to The Championships for three years ended in a 7-6(4), 6-7(6), 5-7, 1-6 defeat to Lucas Pouille, while Nick Kyrgios earned a fourth-round meeting with Andy Murray by beating Feliciano Lopez 6-3, 6-7(2), 6-3, 6-4. Kyrgios and Murray are good friends. "It's just good to have one of the best players in the world, to have a good friend like that," Kyrgios said. When asked how they first became friends Kyrgios smiled and said it was "love at first sight".

Kyrgios was asked about a rant towards his entourage during the match, later insisting that he was "not meaning to be rude or disrespectful" and that it had been said "in the heat of battle".

Tomas Berdych held off the challenge of 19-year-old Alexander Zverev to win 6-3, 6-4, 4-6, 6-1 in the last match of a memorable day on Centre Court. "To play on Sunday, on this Centre Court, I think it is very special," Berdych said afterwards. "I am one of the guys that really love traditions. This is just the fourth time in such a long history of The Championships that we are playing on the Middle Sunday. I get a chance to play on Centre Court, so it can't be better than that."

Annika Beck was next in line to try and derail the Serena Williams Express, but it was full steam ahead for the defending champion who lost just three games in the match

New roof please!

A splendid view across No.1 Court as Nick Kyrigos takes on Feliciano Lopez. Remember it, because in 2017 the vista will be very different. As soon as The Championships 2016 were concluded, contractors moved in to begin removal of the roof pictured here (there will be no roof at all in 2017) as part of the development programme which will see a retractable roof and a series of other improvements installed on Wimbledon's second show court for the start of The Championships 2019.

19-year-old rising star Alexander Zverev of Germany looked the part on Centre Court, taking No.10 seed Tomas Berdych to four sets

Can someone get that please!

Tomas Berdych saw the funny side when a spectator's phone rang on Centre Court

- **Tomas Berdych didn't turn a hair** when a mobile phone went off on Centre Court just as he was about to serve in his match against Alexander Zverev. The big Czech just kept on bouncing the ball as if nothing had happened and said without looking up: "Your phone's ringing, man." Cue laughter all round.

CHAMPIONSHIPS Middle Sunday NOTEBOOK

- **Middle Sunday delivered an unforgettable experience** for one determined and impulsive tennis fan from America.

  On Saturday morning, Allison Creekmore saw a tweet from a newspaper reporter suggesting that, if anyone in the US was keen enough, they could book a ticket online on Saturday and still have time to jump on a plane and make it to Wimbledon to witness the historic occasion.

  So, on an impulse, that's just what she did. Thrilled to land a Centre Court ticket, she booked a flight from New York at 7pm, landed at London Heathrow at 6.30am on Sunday, travelled to a nearby hotel to drop off her bags and then dashed down to the All England Club to see one of her favourites, Serena Williams, in action.

  "I am a huge tennis fan and it's always been a dream of mine to come to Wimbledon," said Allison. "It might be one of the craziest things I've ever done but it's worth it!"

- **The visitors to Wimbledon on this special Sunday** were left a mite confused when they arrived in the town centre to find a bunch of sports fans milling around and bedecked in blue and yellow

You cannot bee serious!

rather than the traditional purple and green.

It turned out that 3,000 supporters of AFC Wimbledon Football Club had taken to the streets to cheer on the players as they paraded their League Two play-off final trophy, a celebration planned when it was assumed that there would be no tennis.

During the speeches from their open top bus, AFC Wimbledon's commercial director Ivor Heller also revealed how the All England Club had been helping the Kingston-based team with their planning application for a new stadium back in the Wimbledon area.

- **Another John Isner epic** ended with America's marathon man finally getting worn down and beaten by Jo-Wilfried Tsonga 19-17 in the final set of their third-round contest.

  The last set, which went on for two hours and nine minutes, reignited the old questions about whether a tie-break should be introduced in the final set to conclude epics that could end up completely exhausting players. Roger Federer, the sage of the tour, came up with a possible solution. He admitted these lengthy matches were "super cool" and that he couldn't take his eyes off the Tsonga-Isner epic, but added: "Maybe they can make a compromise and make a tie-breaker at 12-all."

DAY 7

MONDAY
4 JULY

N ick Kyrgios' talent was never in doubt from the moment he stunned Rafael Nadal on his debut at The Championships two years ago. The 21-year-old Australian has since made rapid progress up the world rankings, but doubts over his ability to realise his enormous potential remain.

The world No.19's 5-7, 1-6, 4-6 defeat to Andy Murray in the fourth round here and his downbeat comments afterwards served only to reinforce the concerns of those who fear that his career is heading in the wrong direction. Kyrgios described his performance in the last two sets as "pretty pathetic", admitted he goes "a little bit soft" when the going gets tough and indicated that he was nowhere near to finding a coach, despite having gone it alone for more than a year now.

However, there was certainly no shame in losing to Murray, who in the absence of the departed Novak Djokovic underlined his status as the title favourite. Since the start of the Masters 1000 tournament in Rome in May, Murray had lost just one match, to Djokovic in the final of the French Open. This was his ninth successive victory on grass and his 50th at The Championships. It was also his 19th win in the 19 tour-level matches he had played against Australians.

Murray made just six unforced errors in a display of glorious shot-making that featured thunderous cross-court forehands, relentlessly consistent double-handed backhands, skidding slices, exquisite drop shots and lobs and tantalising variations of spin and pace. The world No.2 also served beautifully. He dropped only seven points on serve in the last two sets and did not have to defend a single break point.

Anyone would have struggled to live with Murray in this form, but Kyrgios appeared to lose heart all too quickly. "As soon as I lost the first set, I just lost belief," he admitted afterwards. The Australian's tactics and shot selection were often poor. He came into the net behind poor approaches, giving Murray time to line up his passing shots, and tried too many drop shots or big forehands when he should have been building rallies. John McEnroe, commentating on television, said that "disappointment would be an understatement in describing Kyrgios' effort" and added: "He's got to look in the mirror if he wants to become a top player and win Slams now."

Kyrgios' post-match press conference quickly turned into something akin to a psychoanalysis session. Did he think he was doing all he could to realise his potential? "No." Was that something he wanted to change? "I don't know." What could he do to change? "I don't know. To be honest, I woke up this morning and played computer games. Is that the greatest preparation? I don't know. But it was fun." Does he love tennis? "I don't love the sport, but I don't really know what else to do without it."

Why does he not go out and find a coach? "One week I'm pretty motivated to train and play. I'm really looking forward to getting out there. One week I'll just not do anything. I don't really know a coach out there that would be pretty down for that one."

Murray, who has great affection for Kyrgios, said that his advice to a player who can lose belief and focus in matches would be to "keep your head, concentrate on your side of the court and control what you can". He added: "You can't always control what your opponent's doing or how your opponent's playing, but you can apply yourself to every single point and fight for every point. Don't give up any cheap games or anything like that."

Although Murray said that Kyrgios had time on his side, he added: "There are a few things he needs to improve and get better at. The sooner he does that, the better for him and his career."

Spectators strain every sinew to get their hands on Andy Murray's wristband, thrown into the crowd as part of the No.2 seed's traditional victory celebrations

Murray's reward for victory would be a quarter-final meeting with Jo-Wilfried Tsonga, who was 4-2 up in the first set when Richard Gasquet retired with a back injury. Kei Nishikori also failed to last the distance. The No.5 seed, who pulled out of The Championships 2015 before the second round because of a calf injury, quit against Marin Cilic when trailing 1-6, 1-5 because of a rib problem. Cilic would next face Roger Federer, who eased to a 6-2, 6-3, 7-5 victory over Steve Johnson.

Milos Raonic won a match from two sets down for the first time when he beat David Goffin 4-6, 3-6, 6-4, 6-4, 6-4. The Canadian turned the match around by taking more risks and going for his shots. "I was allowing him to play too much, get too much rhythm," Raonic said. "The points were too long."

Next up for Raonic would be Sam Querrey, who beat Nicolas Mahut 6-4, 7-6(5), 6-4 to reach the singles quarter-finals of a Grand Slam tournament for the first time. The world No.41 said he had been determined to prove that his victory over Djokovic in the previous round had not been a fluke. He also admitted: "After the Novak match, I watched every highlight I could over and over. I enjoyed the hell out of that moment."

Lucas Pouille beat Bernard Tomic 6-4, 4-6, 3-6, 6-4, 10-8 but would have to wait until the next day to find out his quarter-final opponent after the fourth-round match between Tomas Berdych and Jiri Vesely was called off because of fading light with the score at two sets apiece.

The fourth round of the Ladies' Singles produced one of the matches of the tournament as Dominika Cibulkova beat Agnieszka Radwanska 6-3, 5-7, 9-7 to set up a quarter-final meeting with Elena Vesnina, who also won a marathon, beating her fellow Russian Ekaterina Makarova 5-7, 6-1, 9-7. Cibulkova and Radwanska fought toe-to-toe for three hours in a match full of breath-taking rallies. Radwanska saved

a match point at 5-4 in the second set and Cibulkova saved one at 6-5 in the decider. The 27-year-old Slovakian twice failed to serve out for the match but finally did so at the third time of asking. "It was so tough to go through," she said afterwards. "It was just an amazing, amazing match."

The victory presented Cibulkova with a potential dilemma in that she was due to get married on the day of the Ladies' Singles Final five days later. The world No.18 and her fiancé, Miso Navara, who was in the crowd on No.3 Court, had planned the date on the basis that grass was not her best surface. However, her victory in the Aegon International at Eastbourne had been followed by some fine performances at The Championships. "I never saw myself as such a great grass court player," Cibulkova said. "But winning Eastbourne and now, being in the quarter-finals, I would change my mind."

Some fans contacted the All England Club to suggest that if Cibulkova made the final she should get married on Centre Court on the same day. However, the 2014 Australian Open runner-up said she would

Serena Williams **(top)** triumphed over Svetlana Kuznetsova **(left)** while Venus Williams **(above)** reached the Ladies' Singles quarter-finals for the first time in six years

The hottest ticket in town

Magic Monday, Manic Monday... call it what you like, Day 7 of Wimbledon provides one of the greatest days of top-class sporting action anywhere in the world, and as well as thousands of fanatical tennis followers it attracts an A-list cast of entertainment stars and showbiz celebrities. From pop stars to newsreaders, from comedians to football legends, the great and the good flock to Wimbledon to cheer, gasp, sigh and applaud along with everyone else as the action unfolds in front of them. Pictured here arriving for the day are Australian sports legends Shane Warne and Pat Cash (*top*), Bond girl Gemma Arterton (*above, left*), newsreader and AELTC member Sir Trevor McDonald (*above, centre*) and *Strictly Come Dancing* hostess Tess Daly (*right*)

Other famous visitors to Wimbledon in 2016 included model Heidi Klum (*above left*), actor Bradley Cooper (*above, centre*), David Beckham and sons (*above, right*), film star Jude Law (*far left*), comedian Michael McIntyre (*left*) and pop star Niall Horan of One Direction (*below*), who couldn't resist a selfie.

change the date if she won her next match. "If we do have to postpone it, then it will be a dream come true, because nothing better could happen to me in my tennis career," she said. "It's no problem to postpone the wedding by one week – and it would be even more enjoyable."

Venus Williams, at 36 the oldest woman in the tournament, reached the quarter-finals for the first time in six years when she beat Carla Suarez Navarro 7-6(3), 6-4. The five-times champion lost the first three games but soon made her greater weight of shot count to secure a quarter-final meeting with Yaroslava Shvedova, who beat Lucie Safarova 6-2, 6-4 to reach the last eight at The Championships for the first time.

Serena Williams beat Svetlana Kuznetsova 7-5, 6-0 but only after turning the match around following the closure of the Centre Court roof. Kuznetsova, who had beaten Williams at the Miami Open in March, broke serve in the ninth game but then failed to serve out for the opening set. Both players were unhappy with the slippery surface after rain fell on the court and at 5-5 they went off as the roof was closed. When they returned Williams won eight matches in a row to book a quarter-final meeting with another Russian, Anastasia Pavlyuchenkova, who won a battle of the big hitters when she beat Coco Vandeweghe 6-3, 6-3.

In the Gentlemen's Doubles Jamie Murray and Bruno Soares, the Australian Open champions, were on court for four hours and 52 minutes against Mate Pavic and Michael Venus without reaching a result. The match was suspended at 13-13 in the final set because of bad light. Meanwhile Lleyton Hewitt and Jordan Thompson were knocked out by the 2014 champions, Vasek Pospisil and Jack Sock.

Britain's Katie Swan had to retire from her first-round match in the girls' singles against Mariam Bolkvadze because of a leg injury. She was trailing 5-6 in the first set at the time.

Security was visibly stepped up at The Championships 2016 in the wake of recent global events, to ensure not just that every visitor to Wimbledon was completely safe – but that they felt so

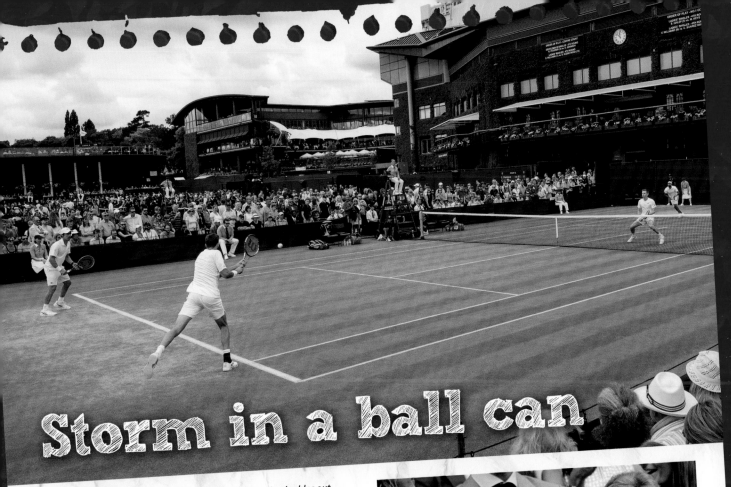

Storm in a ball can

There was no relief during the doubles out on Court 7!

● **There was what you might call a wee spot of bother on Court 7** as Pablo Cuevas and Marcel Granollers lost out in a 26-game fifth set after a dramatic four-hour contest with Jonny Marray and Adil Shamasdin that featured one of Wimbledon's weirder rows – over a bathroom break and a ball can.

During the long fifth set, Cuevas was handed a code violation for unsportsmanlike conduct after threatening to urinate into an empty ball can after he'd been refused permission to leave the court for a bathroom break by the umpire.

He and Granollers later received another code violation after hitting the ball out of the court in frustration and being docked a point, following which they staged a sit-down protest for five minutes, refusing to complete the final game. Order was eventually resumed after a visit from the supervisor but the aggrieved pair were still complaining after losing the final set 12-14.

Still, it must have been quite a relief for everyone when the match ended!

● **On a day when a few top golfers, past and present**, were Royal Box guests, nothing seemed more fitting than Jack Nicklaus, the man who's won the most golf majors (18) watching Roger Federer, the man who's won the most tennis slams (17) take another step towards trying to match his figure.

The great Federer even conceded afterwards that being watched by great sportsmen like Nicklaus was the one thing guaranteed to still induce a bit of trepidation in him.

"That's the only thing that still gets me nervous, when I see people like that sitting watching my match," he said. "I feel like 'Better play well'. You don't want to disappoint legends of sport."

● **Former England cricketer Phil Tufnell** was never the greatest fielder but he surpassed himself the day he dropped an Aussie in the slips at Wimbledon.

Andy Murray was warming up with Nick Kyrgios before their fourth-round match when a ball deflected off the frame of the Australian's racket and shot up towards the Royal Box where 'The Cat', as Tufnell is universally known, must have been in familiar cat-napping mode as he put down a sitter.

Being Tuffers, he could see the funny side – and so could the current England star, a most amused Stuart Broad, nearby.

DAY
8
TUESDAY
5 JULY

When Venus Williams revealed at the 2011 US Open that she was suffering from Sjogren's syndrome, an incurable auto-immune disease that affects energy levels and causes joint pain, could anyone have imagined that five years later, at the age of 36, she would reach her first Ladies' Singles semi-final at The Championships since 2009?

Previous pages: Serena Williams powers her way past Anastasia Pavlyuchenkova to reach yet another Wimbledon semi-final

Those who doubted whether the five-times Wimbledon champion would ever return to the highest levels of a sport she had graced for so many years forgot the unquenchable spirit that has made Williams and her sister two of the greatest athletes of all time. With Venus and Serena winning their quarter-finals against Yaroslava Shvedova and Anastasia Pavlyuchenkova respectively, they were now just one round away from meeting in the Ladies' Singles Final at The Championships for the fifth time. We might have grown accustomed to 34-year-old Serena defying the years, but the progress of her sister, who was the oldest player in the 128-strong Ladies' Singles field at the All England Club, was nothing short of astonishing.

Increasingly troubled by ill health, Venus had played only four tournaments in the 26 months between the 2010 US Open and the 2012 Miami Open, which led to her dropping out of the world's top 100 for the first time in 15 years. The prospect of playing in the 2012 Olympic tournament at the All England Club gave her the motivation to return to competition. After she changed to a vegan diet, adapted her training regime and went on to medication, a super-human effort saw the former world No.1 accumulate enough ranking points to represent her country at the Games for a fourth time. Remarkably, Venus and Serena won their third Olympic Doubles gold at the 2012 Games.

Anyone who thought that might be an appropriate moment for Venus to put away her racket for good was wrong again. Even if she was not the force she had been – she won only one singles title in a four-year spell between 2010 and 2014 – Williams kept on competing. By 2015, when she reached the quarter-finals of the Australian and US Opens and returned to the world's top 10 for the first time since 2011, it was clear that she was determined to remain a contender for the biggest prizes.

Having shown great resilience to come through some testing encounters in her first four matches at The Championships, Williams was simply too good for Shvedova, the world No.96, who led 5-2 in the tie-break but eventually lost 6-7(5), 2-6. Williams, the oldest player to advance to a Grand Slam singles semi-final since 37-year-old Martina Navratilova finished runner-up at The Championships 22 years earlier, was asked to compare her game with 2010, when she had last reached the final four in the singles event at a Grand Slam tournament. "I don't remember – six years ago is ages ago," she laughed. "I think I was most likely kicking butt six years ago if I was in the semis or the finals."

Williams said that even in her most difficult moments she had not contemplated retirement. "Retiring is the easy way out," she said. "I don't have time for easy." She added: "I always felt like I had the game. This is always a plus, when you know you have the game. So you just have to keep working until things fall into place."

The player standing in Williams' path en route to the final would be Angelique Kerber, who beat Simona Halep 7-5, 7-6(2) in a tight contest which featured 13 breaks of serve. The 28-year-old German, the only player yet to drop a set in the tournament, said she was playing as well as she had in January, when she won her maiden Grand Slam title at the Australian Open. That was in marked contrast to her form at the

Far left: Playing her best tennis at Wimbledon for some years, 36-year-old Venus Williams turned back the clock to beat Yaroslava Shvedova

Below: Despite giving it everything and leading 5-2 in the first set tie-break, Shvedova did not have enough to beat the resurgent veteran

The unique Venus

The one and only Venus Ebony Starr Williams not only defied the odds by becoming the oldest singles semi-finalist for 22 years with her victory over Yaroslava Shvedova but also, at 36 and having battled against Sjogren's syndrome, the resurgent, contented five-times champion also delighted everyone at this year's Wimbledon with her mellow thoughts on tennis, the universe and everything.

On her age: "I still feel 26. You have this infinity inside of you that feels like you could go forever. That's how I feel on the court."

On playing at 40: "If I'm at the 2020 Olympics and that's part of the plan, then I'll be there… I'm not into a swan song. When I'm done, it will be done!"

On the 21-year-old Venus: "Well, you have to understand that 21-year-olds are foolish! I didn't think I was going to be here at 36. Now, if I'm here at 46, I will say that 36-year-olds are foolish."

On her tennis: "I just want to get better. When you're an athlete, 'great' is still not enough. You want to be extraordinary and perfect. If you don't reach that, you're not happy."

On retirement: "Well, when you're an athlete, you're not out here thinking about your age. You're thinking about what you can accomplish. Perhaps people will think of it more that way. I'm in a good place."

On what keeps her motivated: "Winning matches. Duh!"

French Open, where she had lost in the first round to Kiki Bertens. "When I arrived in Paris, I was feeling much more pressure," Kerber said. "When I arrived here, I was telling myself, just like in Australia: 'Just be relaxed, play round by round, don't make things too complicated.' I wasn't putting pressure on myself."

Kerber had beaten Serena Williams in the Melbourne final and knew she might have to beat both sisters here to claim her second Grand Slam title. Serena, who in beating Pavlyuchenkova 6-4, 6-4 did not have to defend any break points and hit 11 aces, would be going into her semi-final against another Russian, Elena Vesnina, as the overwhelming favourite.

Whatever the semi-final results, history suggested that either Serena or Venus would go on to win the title. On all 10 previous occasions when the sisters had reached the last four of the same Grand Slam tournament, one of them had gone on to lift the trophy. Might they also add a sixth Wimbledon Ladies' Doubles title? Following their victories in the singles, Venus and Serena returned to court later in the day to beat the Czech Republic's No.6 seeds, Andrea Hlavackova and Lucie Hradecka, 6-4, 6-3 in the third round.

Serena said that she took inspiration from her sister's continuing excellence. "She has a lot of perseverance," the world No.1 said. "She's a great fighter. With everything she's been through, I think it's built a ton of character in her, and in me just by being around her."

Asked about the fact that the two sisters were still playing at the top, 19 years after Venus competed in her first Grand Slam final and 17 years after hers, Serena said: "I'm surprised by the longevity of it. That definitely took me by surprise. When you're younger and you have a dream and you say it and you believe it, that's one thing. But for it to really happen and to come true, it's just a completely different emotion."

Vesnina meanwhile beat Dominika Cibulkova 6-2, 6-2 in what was her first Grand Slam quarter-final in singles. The 29-year-old Russian has enjoyed more success as a doubles player, having won Grand Slam titles at both the French and US Opens playing with Ekaterina Makarova, but her power and consistent ball-striking were too much for Cibulkova, who would at least no longer face a dilemma about whether to postpone her wedding, which she had planned on the day of the final on Saturday.

"I think nothing can be better than playing against Serena in a semi-final on Centre Court at Wimbledon," Vesnina said afterwards. "I'm admiring her. I'm always watching. She's number one in the world. She's the best player in the world. I respect both Serena and Venus. What they bring to the sport is just incredible."

Vesnina said she would try to learn from the example Kerber had set against Serena in the final in Melbourne. "I saw how Angelique was sticking to her game from the first till the last, she was not giving up," Vesnina said. "You have to take your chances against Serena. If she's giving you those chances, you need to be there. If she's serving aces all over the place, hitting winners, there's nothing you can do. You just have to wait and stick with her."

There were 13 breaks of serve in the ding-dong contest between Simona Halep **(top)** and Angelique Kerber **(above)**, with the German ultimately coming out on top

Tomas Berdych completed the Gentlemen's Singles quarter-final line-up when he beat his fellow Czech, Jiri Vesely, 4-6, 6-3, 7-6(8), 6-7(9), 6-3. The match had been suspended in near darkness at the end of the fourth set at 9.21pm the previous evening, after Vesely had saved five match points, and Berdych's request to finish it on Centre Court under the roof and lights was turned down. Berdych might have been reminded of his experience two years previously when he was beaten in the third round by Marin Cilic in a match that ended at 9.38pm, which was the latest ever finish at The Championships away from Centre Court.

However, Berdych was the faster man out of the blocks when they returned for what had become a one-set shoot-out. The world No.8 broke serve in the opening game and did so twice more to secure a quarter-final meeting with France's Lucas Pouille. "It was not really a position I would like to be in, especially last night," Berdych said afterwards. "But the important thing was that I was able to erase it from my mind very quickly, get a good night's sleep, and come back strong again to finish the last set."

Jamie Murray and Bruno Soares, having been on court for nearly five hours the previous day when their third-round Gentlemen's Doubles match against Mate Pavic and Michael Venus was also suspended because of bad light, at 13-13 in the deciding set, needed only 11 more minutes to complete a 6-3, 7-6(3), 4-6, 4-6, 16-14 victory. Bob and Mike Bryan reached the quarter-finals for the 11th year in a row by beating Radek Stepanek and Nenad Zimonjic 7-5, 6-7(10), 6-4, 3-6, 6-3. Meanwhile Britain's Neal Skupski and Anna Smith saved four match points before beating Ivan Dodig and Sania Mirza, the top seeds, 4-6, 6-3, 7-5 in the second round of the Mixed Doubles.

Elena Vesnina was elated to overcome Dominika Cibulkova, allowing her opponent to proceed with her wedding plans for the weekend

Not to be sniffed at

Dominika Cibulkova's talents go beyond reaching Wimbledon quarter-finals

• **Dominika Cibulkova's marvellous winning streak** on grass courts finally came to an end when she ran into Elena Vesnina in the quarter-finals, but the Slovakian still left behind a bit of magic for Wimbledon to remember.

For it turned out that she had a 'super power' that she was prepared to share for the TV cameras. Wearing a blindfold, 'Ci-ball-kova', as she's now bound to be known, took a variety of tennis balls and identified by smell alone the Grand Slam at which that particular sphere was used.

And what enabled her to pick up that particularly useless skill? "I have a good nose," she smiled.

• **There's something magic about Ivan Lendl**, too. After his return to Andy Murray's coaching team, it was noticeable how the Scot then immediately launched into an impressive unbeaten streak that took in another title at The Queen's Club.

Bruno Soares, doubles partner of Andy's brother Jamie, swore that he felt the knock-on effect of Lendl's presence too, tweeting in awe about #thelendleffect.

When Elena Vesnina, mixed doubles partner of Soares, wanted to know what all the fuss was about, he told her: "You'll see..."

Sure enough, in her first competition since then, Vesnina has made a remarkable breakthrough, culminating in her quarter-final victory over doubles partner Ekaterina Makarova.

"You see I've received #thelendleffect too. There's something in it; I'm in the semi-final of Wimbledon!" she beamed after her win.

• **One of the joys of Wimbledon** is to take a short break from the tennis to treat yourself to a punnet of strawberries and cream. The Championships' caterers revealed that, amid the largest single annual sporting catering operation in Europe, overseen by 1,800 staff, they supplied 140,000 portions of English strawberries and 10,000 litres of dairy cream. All washed down, doubtless, by the 29,000 bottles of champagne!

• **Francesca Jones was knocked out** of her second-round girls' match with American teenager Kayla Day, but the young Briton left an indelible mark on The Championships thanks to her extraordinary determination to succeed in the game.

The 15-year-old from Bradford, England, was born with ectrodactyly ectodermal dysplasia syndrome, a rare condition that caused development problems with her hands and feet, leaving her with only three fingers and a thumb on each hand.

Yet despite her right hand – her racket hand – being abnormally small and also having had to overcome difficulties with her balance due to having only seven toes, Francesca has never allowed her condition to thwart her tennis ambitions.

She explained she was proud of the way she had battled on with her successful junior career after a series of operations and added: "I believe I have the level of a top-five player so I'm just going to go for it." Her Yorkshire spirit and talent could take Francesca a long way.

DAY
9
WEDNESDAY
6 JULY

The Championships has staged countless wonderful matches over the years, but has Centre Court ever witnessed a more memorable pair of quarter-finals?

On a day of almost unrelenting drama Roger Federer came back from two sets to love down to beat Marin Cilic 6-7(4), 4-6, 6-3, 7-6(9), 6-3, saving three match points along the way, before Andy Murray, having let slip a two-set lead, finally overcame Jo-Wilfried Tsonga, winning 7-6(10), 6-1, 3-6, 4-6, 6-1. By the end the spectators, let alone the players, must have been exhausted.

Although Federer had reached the quarter-finals with four successive straight-sets victories, nobody could be quite sure of his form and fitness given his physical problems in the first half of the year. Cilic, a fine grass court player who had beaten the Swiss in their most recent meeting in the semi-finals of the 2014 US Open, looked sure to provide a major test.

For two and a half sets Federer struggled to read Cilic's serve. The world No.13 was striking the ball beautifully, hurrying Federer into his shots with the power of his ground strokes. Chances were rare in the first two sets, but Cilic played the big points better and continued to make the running in the third. At 3-3 Federer held serve from 0-40 down and promptly broke in the next game when Cilic double-faulted. When the seven-times Gentlemen's Singles champion served out to take the set the crowd roared their approval.

Federer holds a special place in the affections of the British public and as his comeback gathered momentum the roars grew even louder. Nevertheless, it was Cilic who again set the pace in the fourth set. At 1-2 Federer held serve from 15-40 down as Cilic twice misfired when returning second serves. The Swiss went on to save match points when trailing 4-5 and 5-6 and at 6-7 in the tie-break. Two were on Federer's second serve, but on each occasion he kept his composure.

On his fifth set point, at 10-9 in the tie-break, Federer levelled the match. Now the pendulum had swung the way of the Swiss, who was dictating more of the points. Cilic's resistance finally crumbled when he was broken at 3-4 in the deciding set, upon which Federer served out for victory after three hours and 17 minutes with his 26th and 27th aces. It was the 10th time in his career that he had won from two sets down.

"To win a match like this, to test the body, to be out there again fighting, being in a physical battle and winning it, is an unbelievable feeling," Federer said afterwards. "It was an emotional win. It always is when you come back from two sets to love, but because of the season that I've had it's wonderful. I was just very happy that I actually felt as strong as I did, mentally and physically, when I was down two sets to love.

"I remember just being in trouble the whole time. It just was continuous for an hour or two. After I lost the second set, anything you touch and do is crucial. You cannot afford anything any more."

Federer agreed that the quality of his second serve had been crucial. "I believe in my second serve," he said. "I feel that even if I go bigger, it's still not that much of a risk. That has served me well throughout my career. I think Pete [Sampras] once said: 'You're only as good as your second serve.' I'm happy that my second serve has always been there for me."

Although Federer thought he had "got lucky to some extent" he added: "I fought, I tried, I believed. At the end I got it done."

At 34 years and 336 days, Federer became the oldest man since Ken Rosewall in 1974 to reach the Wimbledon singles semi-finals. His 84th match win at The Championships took him to the top of the list alongside Jimmy Connors, whose record of 11 Wimbledon semi-finals he also equalled, while his 307th win in Grand Slam singles took him one clear of Martina Navratilova's all-time record.

Cilic was striking the ball beautifully and looked to have one foot in the semi-finals

If the Wimbledon public have a bigger hero than Federer it is Murray, who along with Tsonga had the unenviable task of trying to match the drama that had just unfolded on Centre Court. The Scot and the Frenchman rose to the challenge in a match that lasted three hours and 53 minutes. Tsonga had lost 12 of his previous 14 meetings with Murray, including two on Centre Court, but the world No.12 loves to play on grass, on which his huge serves, crunching forehands and sharp volleys are especially effective.

The first set, which featured two early breaks, could not have been tighter. The tie-break tipped one way and then the other until Murray won a wonderful point when Tsonga served at 10-10, cracking a forehand down the line which the Frenchman was unable to return. A volley winner gave the Scot the first set after 76 minutes. He took the second in just 26 minutes, but Tsonga capitalised on a loose service game by the world No.2 early in the third and levelled the match after fighting back from a break down in the fourth.

The only occasion when Murray had lost a match at The Championships from two sets up had been in his debut year in 2005 against David Nalbandian. However, his response on this occasion was more akin to his victory over Novak Djokovic in the 2012 US Open Final, when he recovered from the loss of sets three and four to take immediate command of the decider.

After Murray saved a break point in the opening game, he was heard to shout to his player box: "No way I'm going to lose this match." As he went 5-0 up, the crowd were regularly on their feet, with the exception, of course, of Ivan Lendl, Murray's coach, who sat expressionless throughout. Murray secured his 27th successive victory over Frenchmen at Grand Slam level with an ace. In reaching his seventh singles semi-final at The Championships he equalled the tallies of both Lendl and Djokovic, while his 51st win at Wimbledon matched Bjorn Borg's total. It was also his 100th tour-level victory on grass; Federer, with 152 wins, is the only other currently active player to have won as many.

"I tried to use all of my energy at the beginning of the fifth set to try and get myself up and try and get the crowd pumped up," Murray said. "It had been a long day for them with some long matches. Thankfully I got the early break and managed to hang on."

Far left: Showing incredible resilience and determination, Federer brilliantly clawed his way back from a losing position to record one of his most famous Wimbledon wins

Below: Jo-Wilfried Tsonga was floored by the sheer power and consistency of the tournament's new favourite, Andy Murray

Above: With one notable exception, Murray's box celebrate ecstatically as he powers towards victory

Left: The 2013 Gentlemen's Singles champion kept the crowd pumped up after a marathon day of scintillating action on Centre Court

At his post-match press conference Murray was asked, tongue-in-cheek, how it felt to be "the nation's last hope" given that Britain needed a new prime minister, the England football team needed a new manager and the television programme *Top Gear* was looking for a new presenter. "It's not that bad, is it?" Murray said with a smile. "There are a lot more hopes left than me. I just try my best at this event to make all the people that watch happy."

Murray's victory earned a semi-final meeting with Tomas Berdych after the Czech beat France's Lucas Pouille, who had never previously gone beyond the second round of a Grand Slam tournament, 7-6(4), 6-3, 6-2. Berdych, playing in his 52nd consecutive Grand Slam event, had reached the semi-finals here once before, when he went on to lose to Rafael Nadal in the 2010 final.

Federer's semi-final opponent, for the second time in three years, would be Milos Raonic, who ended Sam Querrey's best run in a Grand Slam tournament with a 6-4, 7-5, 5-7, 6-4 victory. Raonic's confident touch at the net proved crucial. The Canadian followed the advice of John McEnroe, who had joined his coaching entourage at the start of the grass court season. "We focused on not passing up any opportunities to come forward, to always keep the pressure on my opponents, keep them guessing, making them feel uncomfortable," Raonic said. Querrey's big forehand did not fire as effectively as it had when he beat Djokovic in the third round, though he won the third set after converting his first break point of the match.

Jamie Murray and Bruno Soares, the Australian Open champions, had survived a five-set marathon in the third round of the Gentlemen's Doubles but were unable to repeat the feat in the quarter-finals when they were beaten 4-6, 4-6, 7-6(11), 7-6(1), 8-10 by Julien Benneteau and Edouard Roger-Vasselin. Murray and Soares saved three match points in the third set and fought back from two sets down before succumbing after four and a half hours. The defeat meant that Nicolas Mahut would replace Murray at the top of the world doubles rankings the following week. Mahut and Pierre-Hugues Herbert beat Henri Kontinen and John Peers 6-4, 6-7(6), 6-4, 7-6(8).

Elena Vesnina, who was already through to the semi-finals of the Ladies' Singles, reached the quarter-finals of the Ladies' Doubles when she partnered Ekaterina Makarova to a 6-3, 6-4 victory over Michaella Krajicek and Barbora Strycova. Elsewhere, Gabriella Taylor, the last Briton in the girls' singles, survived a suspected viral illness to beat the No.2 seed, Switzerland's Rebeka Masarova, 6-1, 6-1 in just under an hour.

The quarter-finals on Centre Court somewhat overshadowed those on No.1 Court, where Milos Raonic (**right**) overpowered Sam Querrey (**far right**) and Tomas Berdych (**bottom right**) defeated Lucas Pouille (**bottom left**)

Very high five! Petra Kvitova does her best to reach 6ft 10in John Isner's hand

• **After 34 years of cutting and styling the hair** of the great and the good at Wimbledon, Suzanne Strong, who runs the ever-busy Hairdressing Salon and Nail Bar, revealed that this will be her last year in charge.

Yet the popular Suzanne will be back next year to offer help to the new supremo Maria di Gregorio and is wondering if she'll be asked to cut John Isner's hair again.

The 6ft 10in American presented her with a challenge like no other when he popped in. "I couldn't reach the front of his head from behind the chair," Suzanne told wimbledon.com. "We have chairs we can pump up, but I couldn't get it down low enough. I needed a box!"

• **Wimbledon may be a global phenomenon** but the All England Club has worked hard on the important role it can play in improving people's lives in its local community.

So the Wimbledon Foundation, the charity of the AELTC and The Championships established in 2013, was delighted to announce a donation of £10,000 per year over the next two years to continue its support of the Merton night shelter, which keeps homeless people safe and warm during the harsh winter months.

• **Stefan Edberg may have no longer been part of Roger Federer's coaching team** but the two-time Wimbledon champion was still a welcome guest in the great man's Centre Court box during The Championships.

Not that the 50-year-old Swede seems any different to the modest, boyish figure who was such a Wimbledon favourite with his graceful

serve-and-volley game. After Federer's fourth round victory against Steve Johnson, Edberg was spotted taking the tube from Southfields. No courtesy car for tennis' cherished Average Joe.

• **Allis Moss, the new 'voice of Wimbledon'**, had a pretty demanding first week in her role as public address announcer, constantly having to deliver more wretched news to spectators about rain delays. She had to make more than 30 weather announcements in the first six days!

Somehow, though, such was the soothing, mellifluous quality of her voice that only Allis could make it sound as if, actually, things weren't too bad, as she explained: "The referee has decided there will be no further play. Thank you for your patience on what has been a somewhat trying day."

Yet by the second Wednesday and with the weather improving, the former BBC presenter, who gathered a bit of a cult following on social media, even had the chance to pop out of her booth near Centre Court to enjoy watching some tennis there for the very first time.

"This is an experience to aim for at least once if you can," Allis told wimbledon.com. "For me, as a newcomer, the atmosphere is primeval, with the drive to survive, the passion of supporters and the thrills reminiscent, I imagine, of an ancient amphitheatre." Beautifully said again, Allis.

A cut above the rest

DAY
10

THURSDAY
7 JULY

S erena and Venus Williams had been on course to meet in the Ladies' Singles Final at The Championships for the fifth time in their careers, but it was not to be. Instead the younger of the sisters would face a rematch of a different kind.

For the second time in six months Serena would play a Grand Slam singles final against Angelique Kerber, who had beaten her to the title at the Australian Open in January and was simply too good for the elder Williams sister here in the semi-finals. Kerber beat Venus 6-4, 6-4, while Serena crushed Elena Vesnina 6-2, 6-0.

Kerber had struggled to replicate the form that earned her a first Grand Slam title in Melbourne on a regular basis, but at The Championships she had rediscovered the consistent excellence that had secured her triumph Down Under. The world No.4 played a smart game against Venus, pulling the American from side to side with some potent hitting from both flanks. An outstanding mover who retrieves more balls than most, Kerber had the better of the baseline exchanges and did a good job of restricting her opponent's forays to the net.

The only part of the 28-year-old German's game that did not look in tip-top shape was her serve, which was broken three times in the opening set as she made a nervous start. Williams, however, looked in even greater trouble on her own serve, which had so often been a key factor in her past successes. The five-times champion did not hit a single ace and did not hold her serve until the fifth time of asking.

Kerber was the youngest of the semi-finalists, whose average age, at 31 years and nine months, was the highest at a Grand Slam event in the Open era by 18 months. At 36 Williams was the oldest woman to reach the semi-finals of a Grand Slam singles competition since 1994. On this occasion the years finally seemed

Above: The Duchess of Cambridge and All England Club Chairman Philip Brook show their appreciation for a thrilling match, while Williams and Kerber show their respect for each other at the net (below)

to catch up with her. Playing her first singles semi-final at The Championships for seven years, she looked increasingly weary in the second set, in which she made a succession of uncharacteristic errors.

Having taken the first set despite an edgy start, Kerber broke in the opening game of the second and then held to love to go 2-0 up. Williams finally found a better rhythm on her serve, but the damage had been done. Kerber converted her first match point with a forehand winner as she served out for the match after just 71 minutes. She had reached the final without dropping a set in her six matches.

"I knew that Venus had played some long matches, in the first week especially, so I was trying to move her around," Kerber said afterwards. "That is always the plan when you play against Venus because when she has the ball on her racket she just hits it from left to right and you just run. That was my plan, to be the one who was aggressive. I was also returning her serve very well. When she hits her serve, sometimes you have no chance of getting it back."

Kerber became the first German woman to reach the Ladies' Singles Final at The Championships since her childhood idol, Steffi Graf, won the last of her seven Wimbledon singles titles 20 years earlier. Having stopped Serena equalling Graf's Open era record of 22 Grand Slam singles titles at the Australian Open, she would have another chance to do so here.

The German said she had been on a learning curve since winning in Melbourne. "After Australia there were a lot of things to handle, but it's six months ago now," she said. "I learned from this experience. I learned from my ups and downs. I know how to handle everything off the court. I know that I have to take the time for my practice and focus on my work in the gym and on my tennis.

"That's why I'm feeling more relaxed here and I'm not making things too complicated. I have much more experience right now. It was not my first semi-final in a Grand Slam, though Wimbledon is always special. I'm feeling good right now, but that was why I was a little bit nervous when I went out there."

Asked what had turned her from a consistent top 10 player into a serious contender for Grand Slam

honours, Kerber said: "I told myself that I would like to play better in the big tournaments. I think that's what has changed. I just believe much more in myself, especially after Australia. I believe in my game and my team. I'm a little bit more relaxed when I go to tournaments. I know that I can trust my tennis."

Williams said she had simply run into a better player on the day, but would take great encouragement from her performances. "I played a lot of great tennis, a lot of matches," she said. "I was steps away from making it to the end. That's the position I want to be in, playing in the semi-finals, playing for a space in the final. That's what I want. So I take a lot of positives, for sure."

Would she be back in 2017 for her 20th appearance at The Championships? "I would love to. It's all in the plans." She added: "In life there is no such thing as impossible. It's always possible. That's what you feel as an athlete. Pretty much our job is to make the impossible happen every day. It's like magic."

Williams said she would give her sister "a few pointers" for her final against Kerber but added: "For the most part, she's got to go out there and play the match she wants to play, not that I want her to play."

Serena's victory over Vesnina was brutal. At 48 minutes it was the shortest semi-final at The Championships in the Open era, beating Venus' victory over Dinara Safina in 2009 by three minutes. Vesnina was outhit and outmanoeuvred as Williams dropped only three points on her serve to win in record time. The 29-year-old Russian, who looked leaden-footed in the face of such power, won only five points in the second set. "I felt like I had no chance today," the world No.50 admitted afterwards.

The victory put Williams into her third Grand Slam singles final of the year. "For anyone else on this whole planet, it would be a wonderful accomplishment," she said. "For me, it's about obviously holding the

Serena Williams' defeat of Elena Vesnina **(top left)** was brutal, the reigning champion dropping just three points on her serve in the whole match

By royal approval

The Duchess of Cambridge was introduced to Britain's newest tennis star, Gordon Reid, during her busy day at the All England Club

Wheelchair tennis has earned plenty of new devotees since first being introduced at Wimbledon 15 years ago, but the sport was given a huge new profile when the inaugural singles championships were launched in front of enthusiastic crowds and under the gaze of the Duchess of Cambridge.

Wimbledon is the last of the Grand Slams to embrace the singles format and the Duchess, watching from the Debenture restaurant balcony, appeared to be enjoying the entertaining fare on Court 17 as Britain's best player, Gordon Reid, beat France's Nicolas Peifer in the quarter-final.

Briefly, Reid, the Australian Open champion, was taken aback by the "surreal" enormity of the occasion. "I think I got a little bit distracted," he said. "The first time I looked up to the balcony there was this bright yellow dress – that was pretty special! The Duchess came out to watch pretty much the whole first set – that was cool."

The 24-year-old left-hander refocused, went on to win in straight sets and admitted he had achieved a lifetime's ambition.

At 13 this promising junior player lost the use of his legs after contracting transverse myelitis, a neurological condition affecting the spinal cord, and though devastated at the thought he may never pick up a racket again, discovered wheelchair tennis, at first playing only for fun until he realised: "I could get pretty good at this."

"It's always been a dream of mine to play singles here," he admitted with a touch of emotion afterwards – and meeting the Duchess made his day. "She was telling me that William plays a bit of tennis," grinned Reid. "He's a lefty as well, so I told her that all the best ones are!"

trophy and winning, which would make it a better accomplishment for me. For me, it's not enough. But I think that's what makes me different. That's what makes me Serena."

Williams was asked what it felt like to be regarded as "one of the greatest female athletes of all time". Williams said she would prefer to be considered "one of the greatest athletes of all time". She was also asked, in the light of her quickfire victory, whether women deserved equal prize money to men, who play over the best of five sets. "Absolutely," Williams told the journalist who had posed the question. "If you happen to write a short article, do you think you don't deserve equal pay as your beautiful colleague behind you?"

Later in the day Vesnina was on the losing side again when she joined forces with Ekaterina Makarova to face the Williams sisters in the quarter-finals of the Ladies' Doubles. The Russians were beaten 6-7(1), 6-4, 2-6. Venus and Serena had reached the semi-finals on five previous occasions and had gone on to win the title each time. This time their semi-final opponents would be Julia Goerges and Karolina Pliskova, who beat the No.2 seeds, Caroline Garcia and Kristina Mladenovic, 7-6(9), 6-3.

With the Olympic tennis tournament in Rio fast approaching, Venus stressed the importance of their run here. "We've played so sporadically the last few years," she said. "It's not easy to come out and play one match, then not play for a year. We've had a chance to build a little bit, starting in Rome, then the French, and coming along here. As a team our goal is to represent the United States the best we can in Rio."

Meanwhile there was double disappointment for Martina Hingis, whose defences of her Ladies' Doubles and Mixed Doubles titles ended in defeat. Timea Babos and Yaroslava Shvedova beat Hingis and Sania Mirza 6-2, 6-4, with Hingis dropping serve twice in the opening set. Later in the day Hingis and Leander Paes were beaten 6-3, 3-6, 2-6 by Henri Kontinen and Heather Watson, who had been given walkovers after their opponents withdrew from both of their previous matches.

France would have new champions in the Gentlemen's Doubles after Julien Benneteau and Edouard Roger-Vasselin secured a meeting with their fellow countrymen, Pierre-Hugues Herbert and Nicolas Mahut, in the final. Benneteau and Roger-Vasselin overcame seeded opponents for the fourth round in a row when they beat Raven Klaasen and Rajeev Ram 7-5, 6-4, 5-7, 7-6(5), while Herbert and Mahut beat Treat Huey and Max Mirnyi 6-4, 3-6, 6-7(3), 6-4, 6-4.

After their earlier exertions, the Williams sisters appear to be enjoying the attention of the crowds as they make their way on to No.2 Court for their early evening doubles match

Things can only get better!

Heather Watson was fined $12,000 for her out of character outburst in the first round

● **Heather Watson said she was "shocked"** by the severity of her $12,000 fine for slamming her racket into the ground in her singles defeat against Annika Beck the previous week – $2,000 more than Viktor Troicki received for his much-publicised screaming rant the previous Thursday.

"I had no previous history, I'm not a maniac on the court, I don't do controversial things consistently or ever really," said Watson in her own defence. But at least her mood was improved by teaming up with Finn Henri Kontinen and knocking out defending champions Leander Paes and Martina Hingis in the Mixed Doubles to reach the quarter-finals

● **Marion Bartoli, the former Ladies' Singles champion**, was given a heartfelt vote of sympathy and support from current holder Serena Williams after she had appeared on a national daytime television show to reveal how a mystery virus had made her weight drop dramatically, left her suffering from severe allergies and forced her out of invitational matches at Wimbledon.

The 31-year-old Frenchwoman, champion in 2013 and at the tournament as a commentator, said her life had been made "a nightmare" after she caught an unknown virus while visiting India earlier in 2016.

It proved so debilitating, she said, that she could not even type on her phone without gloves and had to wash in mineral water. "I wouldn't wish what I am going through on anyone. Maybe my heart will stop. Going through all this is difficult," said Bartoli, who explained she wanted to go public about her problems because of all the false rumours that she was suffering from an eating disorder.

Her plight prompted an outpouring of sympathy from her old opponents. "I was really proud to hear she did say something," said Williams. "She took it upon herself to acknowledge what she's been fighting through. I really admire anyone that is courageous like that."

Gabriella Taylor bravely bowed out of the girls' singles

● **In the girls' singles event**, Britain's last contender, Gabriella Taylor, who had managed to battle through a suspected viral illness the previous day to win her third-round match, had to retire while trailing 4-6, 1-1 against the American, Kayla Day.

DAY
11

FRIDAY
8 JULY

I t had been a long road back, but three years after becoming the first British man to win the Gentlemen's Singles title at The Championships since 1936, Andy Murray earned himself another shot at his sport's greatest prize.

Having made a lengthy recovery from back surgery and recovered from the disappointments of defeats in three subsequent Grand Slam finals, Murray removed Fred Perry's name from another line in the British history books when he beat Tomas Berdych 6-3, 6-3, 6-3 to reach his 11th Grand Slam final. That beat Perry's British record of 10 finals following the abolition of the Challenge Round at The Championships in 1922. In two days' time Murray would meet Milos Raonic, who became the first Canadian man to reach a Grand Slam singles final when he beat Roger Federer 6-3, 6-7(3), 4-6, 7-5, 6-3.

Having reached his third Wimbledon singles final, following his loss to Federer in 2012 and his victory over Novak Djokovic in 2013, Murray promised to savour the occasion. "The older you get you never know how many more chances you will have to play in Grand Slam finals so you want to make the best of any opportunity," he said. Although he had appeared in the final of all four Grand Slam tournaments, Murray said that playing in the final on Centre Court was particularly special. "For British players growing up, and for a lot of the players, this is the biggest competition," he said. "To get to play in front of a home crowd in a Grand Slam final is very, very rare."

Murray had lost in four of his six previous Wimbledon semi-finals but on this occasion there was barely a moment when his victory looked in doubt. Berdych used to be one of the few players who had won more matches against Murray than he had lost, but the Scot had turned the tables in recent times and had won their last four meetings. That included a fiery encounter in the semi-finals of the Australian Open in 2015, when Berdych had just hired Dani Vallverdu as his coach shortly after the Venezuelan, a long-time friend of Murray's, had left the Scot's entourage.

Berdych had made the better start in Melbourne but this time Murray took the first set in just 35 minutes. After an early exchange of breaks, Berdych dropped serve in the eighth game as a pattern emerged, with Murray's pulsating returns putting the 30-year-old Czech under constant pressure.

The start of the second set was tight again, but Murray eventually forced five break-point opportunities and took two of them. There was only one break point in the third set and it was Murray who took it in the fourth game. Whatever Berdych threw at him Murray had the response, as he proved when playing one of the shots of the tournament in the third set. A Berdych drop shot would have been good enough to beat most opponents, but Murray not only chased it down but managed to hit a wonderful winning lob.

Murray said afterwards: "I didn't give up too many errors and made it very difficult for Tomas. It was quite breezy. It was quite tricky on the court today in comparison with the other days, especially at the beginning of the match. It wasn't as easy to play really good tennis."

In reaching the final Raonic would be entering unknown territory for a Canadian man. The only Canadian with experience of a Grand Slam singles final was Eugenie Bouchard, who had finished runner-up at The Championships two years earlier.

With Murray in the mood, Tomas Berdych was always up against it and the result the Centre Court crowd was cheering for never really looked in doubt

However, the world No.8 had been on the verge of making his breakthrough ever since reaching his first Wimbledon semi-final in 2014, when he had lost in straight sets to Federer. Now the 25-year-old Canadian had two more years' experience under his belt, while the Swiss was just a month short of his 35th birthday. Might this be a day when the oft-discussed takeover by a new generation would become reality?

Federer had won all 10 of his previous Wimbledon semi-finals, but saw his run come to an end in a memorable contest full of brilliant attacking play. Raonic proved that there is much more to his game than a big serve. He hit some stunning ground strokes and attacked the net with the renewed confidence that John McEnroe had brought to his game since joining his entourage at the start of the grass court season. Federer, nevertheless, playing his second successive five-set match on Centre Court, went desperately close to reaching his 11th Centre Court final.

Having served superbly in his earlier matches, Federer now faltered at crucial moments. The only break of the first set came when he double-faulted – for just the third time in the whole tournament – on break point in the fourth game. However, that was Raonic's only break point in the first three sets, while Federer was making increasing inroads into the Canadian's service games. Raonic's double fault at 3-3 was the turning point of the second-set tie-break and his mishit backhand gave Federer the only break of the third set.

The momentum appeared to be with Federer, but Raonic clung on in the fourth set, at the end of which the match turned. To gasps and groans from the crowd, most of whom were willing on Federer, the Swiss hit two double faults in a row when he served at 5-6 and 40-15. He then saved two set points before Raonic levelled the match by drilling a backhand winner down the line.

Federer sent for the trainer to have his right leg massaged and needed further treatment after suffering a heavy fall at 1-2 in the deciding set. The former world No.1 turned his ankle at the end of a stunning rally which had ended with Raonic hitting a forehand cross-court winner. Seeing Federer sprawled full length on the ground and then walking gingerly back to his chair were not images we would normally associate with arguably the greatest player in history.

Far right: Having looked dead and buried during the fourth set, like the whole of Centre Court Raonic could barely believe it when he levelled the match at two sets all

Below: So rarely injured in his career, the sight of Roger Federer on the ground – having turned his ankle during the deciding set – was as uncharacteristic as his first ever Wimbledon semi-final defeat

Although Federer did not appear to be suffering physically when he resumed, the game ended with Raonic hitting a forehand cross-court winner on his second break point. Raonic held serve comfortably thereafter, went 40-0 up after three big serves at 5-3 and converted his first match point when Federer hit a forehand long.

As the players walked off Federer appeared to linger on Centre Court, taking in the scene. He was asked later if that had been an indication that he was wondering whether it might be his last appearance on the stage of so many of his greatest triumphs. However, Federer insisted he had every intention of returning and said he had simply wanted to acknowledge the crowd's great support. "I was fortunate enough to play all my matches on Centre Court," he added. "I don't take that for granted."

Asked what had happened when he dropped his serve from 40-15 up at 5-6 in the fourth set, Federer said: "Something went wrong. I can't believe I served a double fault twice. That's unexplainable for me really. I was very sad about that and angry at myself, because I should never have allowed him to get out of that set that easily."

Raonic said: "I persevered. I was plugging away. I was struggling through many parts of the match. He gave me a little opening towards the end of the fourth. I made the most of it. Then I tried to run away with it. I did a lot of things well. The attitude kept me in the match. I think that's what made the biggest difference. I was quite vocal, but I was always positive."

Left: Sporting to the last, Roger Federer congratulates his opponent after a truly thrilling match

Below: His victory in just less than three and a half hours meant Milos Raonic became the first Canadian man ever to reach a Grand Slam singles final

"I'll be back!"

The Championships always takes a deep sigh when the great Roger Federer departs the scene, but after his semi-final defeat to Milos Raonic there was almost an end-of-an-era feel as the great Swiss champion left his Centre Court kingdom, admitting to feeling angry with himself and very sad.

Such was the prevailing mood that one journalist even asked him whether he felt it might have been his last time on Centre Court and Federer's indignation was a relief for everyone as he responded: "Yes, I hope to be back on Centre Court, to be very clear for you."

That was just what his crestfallen fans around the world needed to hear. Back in Dallas, Colleen Taylor, one of his 'super fans', was at work, trying to follow the live scores with an increasing sense of despair.

Down the years, she has followed him with a passion, hoisting the famous 'Shhh!! Quiet! Genius At Work' banner at big events and even being given the coveted job among the most fervent Federophiles of being the 'courier' who at the start of a tournament hands him the 'Red Envelope' containing all their messages of support.

"Roger may never win another major. I've accepted that," she said. "But as long as he keeps giving himself a chance, I'll be there with him. No doubt I'll die a thousand deaths every time he has matches like the Cilic and Raonic ones, but I'll be with him because I have no choice – I love Roger Federer.

"Will he be back next year? I have no doubt. Roger loves tennis and he loves Wimbledon. And it wouldn't surprise me one iota if Roger found himself in the final next year and won. No surprise at all."

The sun sets on Court 19, as the last match ever to be played there enters its third and final set, the honour falling to Olesya Pervushina and Anastasia Potapova of Russia, who beat Eleni Christofi (Greece) and Lucie Kankova (Czech Republic) in the girls' doubles. The much-loved court must sadly make way for the redevelopment of No.1 Court, due for completion in 2019

Meanwhile Venus and Serena Williams reached their sixth Ladies' Doubles Final at The Championships with a hard-fought 7-6(3), 6-4 win over Julia Goerges and Karolina Pliskova. The sisters clinched victory by winning five games in a row from 4-1 down in the second set. Timea Babos and Yaroslava Shvedova won the second semi-final, beating Raquel Atawo and Abigail Spears 6-4, 6-2.

Shvedova narrowly failed to reach a second final, this time in the Mixed Doubles. Robert Farah and Anna-Lena Groenefeld beat Shvedova and Aisam Qureshi 6-4, 2-6, 7-5. In the other half of the draw Britain's Heather Watson and Finland's Henri Kontinen followed up their victory over Leander Paes and Martina Hingis, the defending champions, by beating Scott Lipsky and Alla Kudryavtseva 6-3, 6-2 in the quarter-finals. The win earned a semi-final meeting with Oliver Marach and Jelena Ostapenko, who beat Juan-Sebastian Cabal and Mariana Duque-Marino 7-5, 4-6, 6-0.

The top two seeds in the boys' singles both went out in the semi-finals. Denis Shapovalov beat Stefanos Tsitsipas 4-6, 7-6(5), 6-2, while Alex De Minaur beat Ulises Blanch 6-3, 6-2. In the girls' singles Dayana Yastremska knocked out the No.1 seed, Olesya Pervushina, winning 7-6(4), 6-7(2), 6-3. In the other semi-final Anastasia Potapova beat Kayla Day 5-7, 6-2, 6-0.

Britain's Gordon Reid beat the No.2 seed, Joachim Gerard, 7-6(9), 6-4 to reach the final of the inaugural Gentlemen's Wheelchair Singles event. Stefan Olsson beat Stephane Houdet, the No.1 seed, 3-6, 6-3, 6-3 in the other semi-final. In the Ladies' Wheelchair Singles semi-finals the top seed, Jiske Griffioen, beat Marjolein Buis 6-7(1), 6-0, 7-6(3), while Aniek Van Koot beat Jordanne Whiley 7-5, 6-3.

Flying the flag for Canada

Rising young Canadian star Denis Shapovalov reached the boys' singles final to mirror the success of his compatriot and inspiration, Milos Raonic

● **Milos Raonic's triumph** that set up the sight of a Canadian man appearing in a Grand Slam singles final for the first time prompted a wave of delight back home, even in the most elevated circles.

Indeed, it was the Canadian Prime Minister Justin Trudeau who led the tributes to the No.6 seed, sending a message on Twitter that read: "Another game for Milos! First Canadian man to make a Grand Slam singles final – one more to go. Good luck on Sunday. #Wimbledon."

● **Raonic wasn't the only Canadian success story, though**. In the boys' singles event, 17-year-old Denis Shapovalov, who hails from Richmond Hill, Ontario, where Raonic also first honed his game, beat top seed Stefanos Tsitsipas, of Greece, 4-6, 7-6(5), 6-2 on Court 12 to reach the final.

Shapovalov, a leftie with a touch of flair and a nice one-handed backhand, is tipped for a rosy future and is grateful to Raonic for being the torchbearer for a prospective new generation of Canadian stars.

"I look up to Milos. He's my inspiration. Before that, there were not many Canadians doing as well as he was," said the youngster, who was born in Israel to Russian parents before the family moved to Canada when he was nine months old.

"For sure it brings hope into my eyes. I hope to be like him one day."

● **An Andy Murray-Milos Raonic showdown**, set up by their semi-final wins, had a few of the older members of the press corps

rubbing their hands in glee as they realised it would also mean a renewal of one of tennis' all-time great rivalries between Ivan Lendl and John McEnroe, only this time as 'super coaches'.

How did they get on as players? Well, you could perhaps glean an idea in an interview that Murray's coach Lendl gave to the BBC, revealing that he had met Raonic's new coaching advisor in the locker room during the tournament.

"Was it a long chat?" the reporter asked, to which Lendl, at his deadpan best, responded: "I didn't say we chatted..."

● **Gordon Reid created a piece of history** by earning a place in the inaugural Gentlemen's Wheelchair Singles Final at The Championships, defeating No.2 seed Joachim Gerard 7-6(9), 6-4 in the semi-finals.

Yet though he was proud of his achievement, Reid was just as delighted at seeing the impact that his sport was making around the grounds.

"Even this week, some people had doubts about how it was going to look, that it was going to be awful and nobody would want to watch it," he said.

"But I think we've proved so far that people are loving to watch the singles. The standard is really high and I think everyone's just really happy we're playing singles here."

DAY
12
SATURDAY
9 JULY

I f at first you don't succeed, try, try again. The origins of that maxim are uncertain, but Serena Williams followed it to the letter as she finally achieved her goal of equalling Steffi Graf's Open era record of 22 Grand Slam singles titles.

Having lost in the finals of both the Australian and French Opens, the 34-year-old American reached Graf's milestone at the third attempt by beating Angelique Kerber 7-5, 6-3 in one of the best Ladies' Singles finals at The Championships in recent years. Kerber, who had beaten Williams in the final in Melbourne, fought hard to defend her childhood idol's record for a second time, but Williams played with the belief of someone who knows how to win on Centre Court.

A seventh Wimbledon singles title put Williams level with Graf and Dorothea Lambert-Chambers and left just two players ahead of her on the all-time list of Wimbledon Ladies' Singles champions. Martina Navratilova won the title nine times between 1978 and 1990, while Helen Wills-Moody won it eight times between 1927 and 1938. Their records will be among the next within Williams' reach, as will Margaret Court's all-time record of 24 Grand Slam singles titles. Patrick Mouratoglou, Williams' coach, is setting the target high. "Serena doesn't equal records," he said after her latest victory. "She beats them."

Some of the media focus going into the final had been on Williams' three "failures" since winning Wimbledon the previous summer. She had lost to Roberta Vinci in the semi-finals of the US Open and to

Kerber and Garbiñe Muguruza respectively in the finals of the Australian and French Opens. Until the latter two defeats Williams had won 21 of the 25 Grand Slam singles finals she had contested. Was her aura of invincibility starting to weaken?

Williams, however, preferred to emphasise her achievements, which included reaching her third successive Grand Slam final. Just like Andy Murray, in fact. "I had to start looking at positives, not focusing on that one loss per tournament, which really isn't bad," she said. "Anyone else on this tour would be completely happy about it. Once I started focusing more on the positives, I realised that I'm pretty good. Then I started playing a little better."

Mouratoglou had noticed a change in Williams' mindset following the French Open and had told her that she sounded like "the real Serena" again. Williams said: "One day I woke up and I just felt different. It's weird. I felt a relief. It was like: I'm not going to worry about anyone or anything. I'm just going to worry about tennis."

Kerber, meanwhile, had put some post-Melbourne troubles behind her to reach the final with six successive straight-sets victories. No German woman had claimed the title since Graf won it for the last time in 1996, but the world No.4 could take confidence from her victory over Williams at the start of the year. On that occasion the 28-year-old German had repeatedly frustrated Williams by forcing her to play the extra ball, but on the quicker surface here she knew she would need to attack first wherever possible.

The match-up made for a spectacular encounter, with both women going for their shots in a succession of hard-fought rallies. Williams always looked to get into the net, where she volleyed effectively, while Kerber was more at home hitting from the baseline. When the rallies got going it was hard to choose between the two women, but on serve the American had a distinct edge.

Williams, who finished with 13 aces, hit her first serves at speeds of up to 124mph and at an average of 109mph (compared with Kerber's figures of 106mph and 93mph respectively), dropped only five of 43 points played on her first serve and had to defend just one break point in the match – which she saved with an ace at 3-3 in the second set. Kerber, meanwhile, did not hit any aces, was under frequent pressure on her serve and faced six break points.

Serena Williams was simply unstoppable, achieving close to perfection in everything she did

Left: The moment Williams won the first set, finally breaking Kerber in the 12th game

Above: Williams collapses to the ground in celebration after her volley winner

Overleaf: Serena Williams holds the Venus Rosewater Dish aloft for the seventh time

Make room for a champion

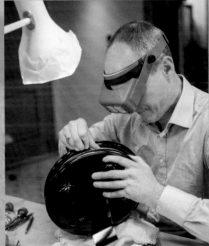

Expert engraver Emmet Smith gets to work on the brand new plinth

After 129 years of presenting the Venus Rosewater Dish to the winner of the Ladies' Singles Final at Wimbledon, last year the All England Club found itself with a problem. Having had the name of each year's winner engraved on to the famous trophy since 1886, first on the front and then the back, after adding "2015 Miss S. Williams" there was no room left for any more names.

In 2016, therefore, Serena Williams' was the first name to go on to a stunning new plinth, designed and made by renowned silversmith Colin Hellier to perfectly complement the historic trophy on which it will sit.

As soon as Williams hit her winning volley to seal victory over Angelique Kerber, engraver Emmet Smith sprang into action in a quiet room in the Centre Court building and began to work his craft. Within half an hour the winner's name was immaculately etched in history, all ready for the ensuing celebrations.

It will be a few more years before anyone at the All England Club has to worry about what to do when the plinth becomes full.

One break in each set was enough to give Williams victory. Kerber had already saved four break points before Williams forced two set points in the 12th game, the second of which she took with a booming forehand. At 3-4 in the second set Kerber dropped serve after leading 40-15. In the next game three unreturned serves put Williams 40-0 up and a volley winner delivered the title, after which the American fell on her back in celebration.

Kerber said that Williams had served "unbelievably", and added: "I think we both played at a really high level. Of course I'm disappointed, but at the end I'm also proud of what I did. I reached my second Grand Slam final this year and it was an amazing final. I really enjoyed it. There was a great atmosphere out there."

Williams said that the 12 months since winning her sixth Wimbledon title had not been easy. "I've definitely had some sleepless nights, if I'm just honest, with a lot of stuff – coming so close, feeling it, not being able to quite get there," she said.

She said that in the immediate future she would not be setting herself new goals – "One thing I learned about last year is to enjoy the moment" – but admitted that the only time she would not feel under pressure would be when she stopped playing. "I think the pressure I put on myself is more than anyone," she said. "I put so many expectations on myself. I expect to win every time I step out on the court. Anything less is unacceptable for me. I think that's just rare and it's different. But it's me. And it's why I have 22 Grand Slam titles."

Mouratoglou could also take some of the credit. Before she joined forces with the Frenchman in 2012, Williams had won 13 of the 47 Grand Slam tournaments she had played. Since then, she had won nine out of 17, a rate of return similar to Court's over the whole span of the Australian's career. Court, who retired at 33, won 24 of the 47 Grand Slam tournaments she contested; Graf, who quit at 30, played 55 Grand Slam tournaments and won 22 of them; Williams, who was still going strong at 34, had won 22 out of 64.

Asked what it felt like to be an inspiration to millions of young girls around the world, Williams said: "That's why I ultimately feel like I'm here. I've been given such a great opportunity. I've been given so much talent. I've been put in a position where I can inspire females, ladies – and men as well. Anyone, any kid out there that wants to be something has dreams. I've had great dreams. I didn't come from any money or anything, but I did have a dream and I did have hope. That's really all you need."

Williams ended a perfect day by joining forces with her sister, Venus, to win the Ladies' Doubles title for the sixth time. Their 6-3, 6-4 victory over Hungary's Timea Babos and Kazakhstan's Yaroslava Shvedova extended two remarkable sequences. The sisters have played in 14 Grand Slam doubles finals together and won them all, while every time they have

Far right: With the ball boys and girls providing the traditional guard of honour, the two finalists leave Centre Court to a tumultuous ovation

Below: The friendship and respect between the two finalists evident after the match was a delight to see

won the doubles at The Championships one of them has also won the singles title. Asked if she ever got bored of winning titles, Serena said: "No, it doesn't get boring. As long as I'm winning, it doesn't get boring. Even when I'm not winning, it doesn't because it makes me want to work harder so I can come out and hold up titles."

Nicolas Mahut and Pierre-Hugues Herbert won the Gentlemen's Doubles title for the first time, beating Julien Benneteau and Edouard Roger-Vasselin 6-4, 7-6(1), 6-3 in the first all-French Grand Slam men's doubles final of the Open era. The champions got together at the start of 2015 and clicked instantly, reaching the final of the Australian Open and winning the US Open. Mahut, who knocked Herbert out of the singles here, secured a return to the No.1 position in the world doubles rankings with his performances at The Championships.

Mahut said that winning the Wimbledon title was "a dream come true". He added: "I said since I started playing tennis that Wimbledon is the greatest tournament. When you win the match point in the final, you just realise that you're going to have your name written on the trophy and everywhere."

Britain's Heather Watson and Finland's Henri Kontinen reached the final of the Mixed Doubles when they beat Austria's Oliver Marach and Latvia's Jelena Ostapenko 7-6(1), 6-3. Colombia's Robert Farah and Germany's Anna-Lena Groenefeld had already booked their places in the final. Kontinen and Watson had never played together until this tournament, while Watson became the first British woman to reach the Mixed Doubles final since Jo Durie won the title alongside Jeremy Bates in 1987.

Russia's Anastasia Potapova took the girls' title, beating Ukraine's Dayana Yastremska 6-4, 6-3 in the final. However, she needed seven match points to secure her victory. Potapova twice celebrated what she thought were title-winning shots only to be denied by successful Hawk-Eye challenges by her opponent. The 15-year-old Russian comes from a family with a notable sporting background, her mother and grandmother having played volleyball and basketball respectively for Russia.

Girl power!

Day 12

A-listers and friends of Serena, Beyoncé (left) and Jay-Z (right) enjoy the view from the players' box

● **There are A-list celebrities** and then there are those of the A* variety. So it was when US superstar Beyoncé, with her other half Jay-Z, turned up in Serena Williams' box for the final, attracting almost as many admiring glances as the brilliant tennis.

The pop megastar and Serena are firm friends, with the champion even taking a starring role in the singer's visual album, *Lemonade*. Only champagne was the order of the day when the queen of showbiz saluted the queen of tennis.

And seeing as she was due on stage in Dublin that very evening, Beyoncé would have been pleased that Serena managed to get the job done in straight sets!

● **Serena Williams' seventh Wimbledon triumph** reheated the old question about whether she just might be the best player of all time, but even after winning her 22nd Grand Slam singles title, equalling Steffi Graf's Open era record, she still has a lot of work to do to beat the 73-year-old who was admiring her play from the Royal Box.

The Rev. Dr Margaret Court, who these days is a Christian minister in Perth, Australia, is now the only player left for Serena to catch, having won 24 Grand Slam singles titles in a career that spanned the amateur and Open game.

An equally distinguished visitor to the Royal Box, six-times Wimbledon champion Billie Jean King enjoyed meeting up with her old rival Court and noted after Serena's awesome victory: "Margaret is on 24 so if Serena can keep her motivation, maybe she'll beat that and maybe she'll be our greatest ever."

Nicolas Mahut (right) and Pierre-Hugues Herbert relished their Gentlemen's Doubles Final win

● **Nicolas Mahut already had his name enshrined** at Wimbledon for his part in the endless 2010 clash with John Isner on Court 18, where a plaque now stands in the players' honour, but the Frenchman always wanted to be remembered for something more than that.

And after his Gentlemen's Doubles triumph with compatriot Pierre-Hugues Herbert, perhaps he will. "It's something special, having my name on the Court 18. I'm very proud of it. But now it's something different, now I can come in the press conference as a Wimbledon champion!"

Yes, rather that than being the man who lost 68-70 in the final set!

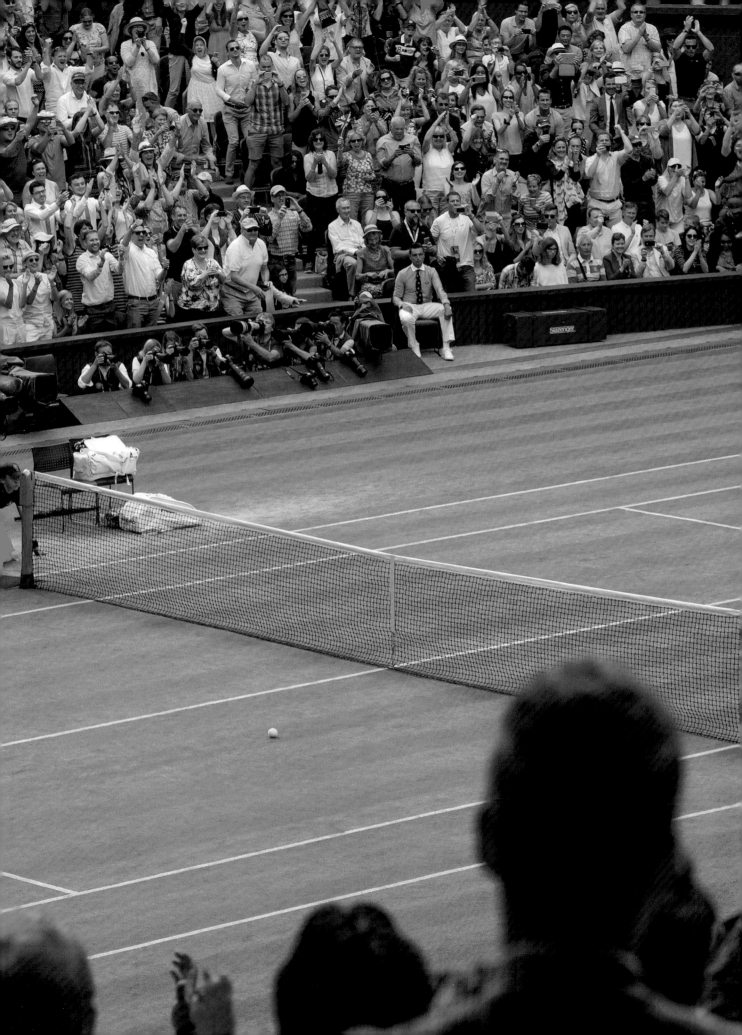

5.00
PREVIOUS SETS

ROLEX

2.47

SETS GAMES POINTS

4 6	Milos RAONIC	0 6 2
3	v	
6 7	Andy MURRAY	2

CHALLENGES REMAINI
M. RAONIC
A. MURRAY

wimbledon.com

DAY
13
SUNDAY
10 JULY

138 mph

Andy Murray had already played in 10 Grand Slam singles finals, including two at The Championships, but as the Scot prepared to face Canada's Milos Raonic he knew that this could be a very different experience.

Previous pages: He's done it! Andy Murray drops his racket, turns to his box and pumps his fist in the air in triumph at the moment he secures his second Wimbledon title

Above: The battle for supremacy in the 2016 Gentlemen's Singles Final was always going to be between Milos Raonic's jet-propelled serve and Andy Murray's return

In all of his previous finals, which had produced just two victories, at the US Open in 2012 and here at the All England Club the following year, Murray had only ever faced Roger Federer or Novak Djokovic and had always been the lower-ranked player. Now, for the first time, the 29-year-old Scot would be the clear favourite. Raonic, the world No.9, was playing in his first Grand Slam final and had lost his five previous meetings with Murray, most recently in the grass court final at The Queen's Club just three weeks previously.

"Obviously it will be the first time I'll play a Slam final against someone that isn't Roger or Novak, so that's different," Murray said. "But you never know how anyone's going to deal with the pressures of a Slam final. I just have to go out there, concentrate on my side, do what I can to prepare well for it and see what happens."

Although this would be his third Grand Slam final in succession following his defeats to Djokovic at the Australian and French Opens, Murray insisted: "It never feels normal. I never take it for granted. I know how difficult it is to make the finals of these events and how hard they are to win."

Murray was unbeaten in 11 successive matches on grass since Ivan Lendl had begun his second spell as his coach the previous month, but the best run of his career dated further back than that. In his last four

tournaments Murray had won the Masters 1000 in Rome and the Aegon Championships, and finished runner-up, to Djokovic, at both the Madrid Masters 1000 and the French Open.

For Raonic, the defeat at Queen's was actually a source of encouragement. In his first outing since asking John McEnroe to join his coaching entourage, the 25-year-old Canadian had shown rapid improvements and had continued to develop his game over the Wimbledon Fortnight. The Queen's final, moreover, had been close, Raonic having led by a set and a break until Murray turned the match around by breaking for the first time with a typically brilliant backhand return winner off a first serve. Raonic might also have been aware of the last time that the same players contested the finals at both Queen's and The Championships; in 1988 Stefan Edberg lost to Boris Becker at Queen's but turned the tables on his great rival at the All England Club three weeks later.

Meanwhile the final was being seen in some quarters as a renewal of the rivalry between Lendl and McEnroe. Murray, nevertheless, said that any interest in that aspect of the final would come from the media rather than the players. "I'm playing against Milos, I'm not playing against John, and Milos isn't playing against Ivan," he said.

However, just as McEnroe had brought extra dimensions to Raonic's game, so Murray was clearly benefiting from the return of Lendl, who had been his coach when he won his two previous Grand Slam titles. "I obviously had the best years of my career with him," Murray said. "The rest of the team working with me has helped get me into this position, but I obviously wanted to work with Ivan again to try to help me win these events. That's the goal."

The key to the match was likely to be how Murray, one of the best returners in tennis, would cope with Raonic's cannonball serves. The answer was already becoming clear before Raonic hit a 147mph first serve –

It was the Murray return that won the day, the Scotsman dealing with everything his Canadian opponent could throw at him... and then some

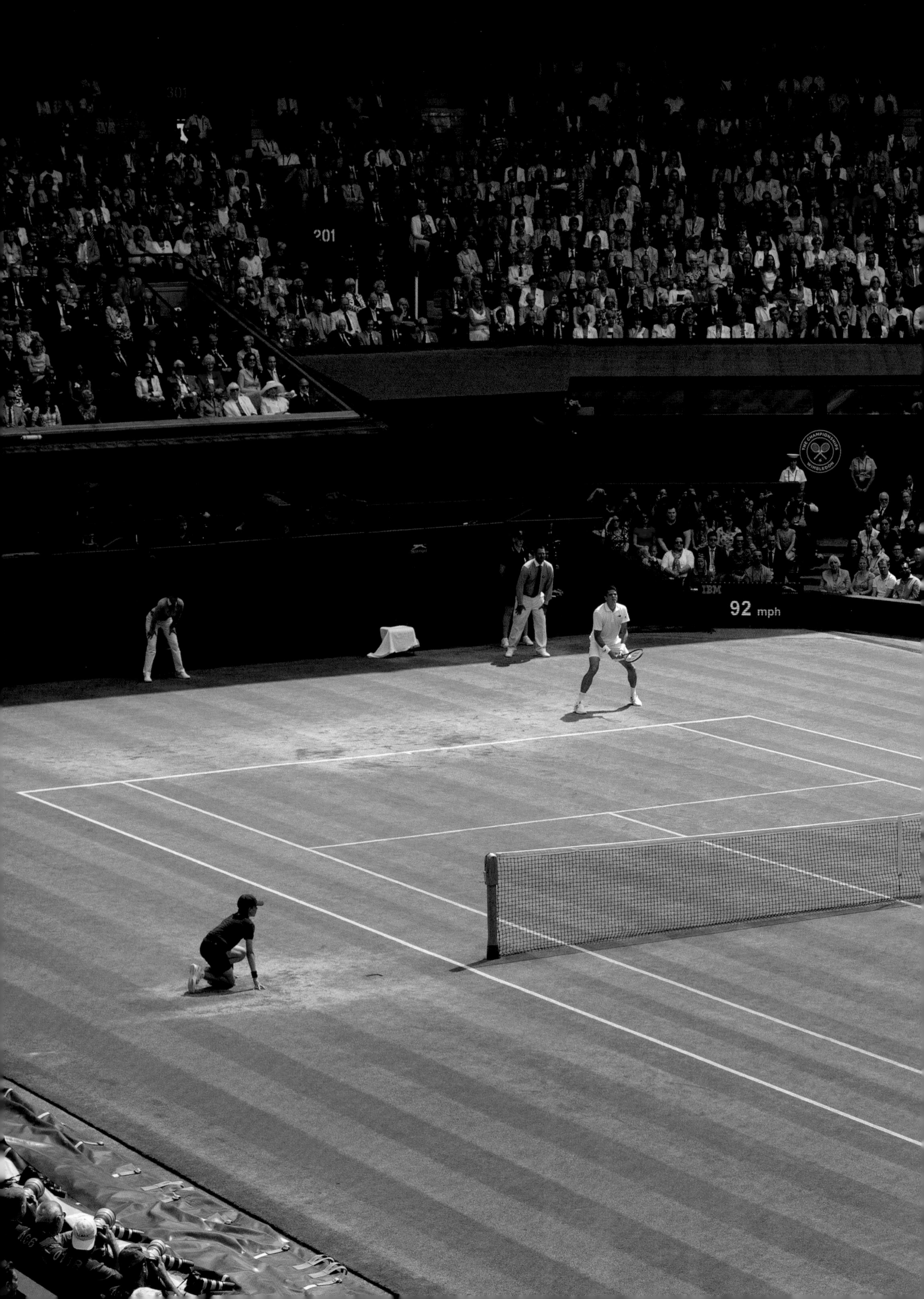
301
201
THE CHAMPIONSHIPS
WIMBLEDON
IBM
92 mph

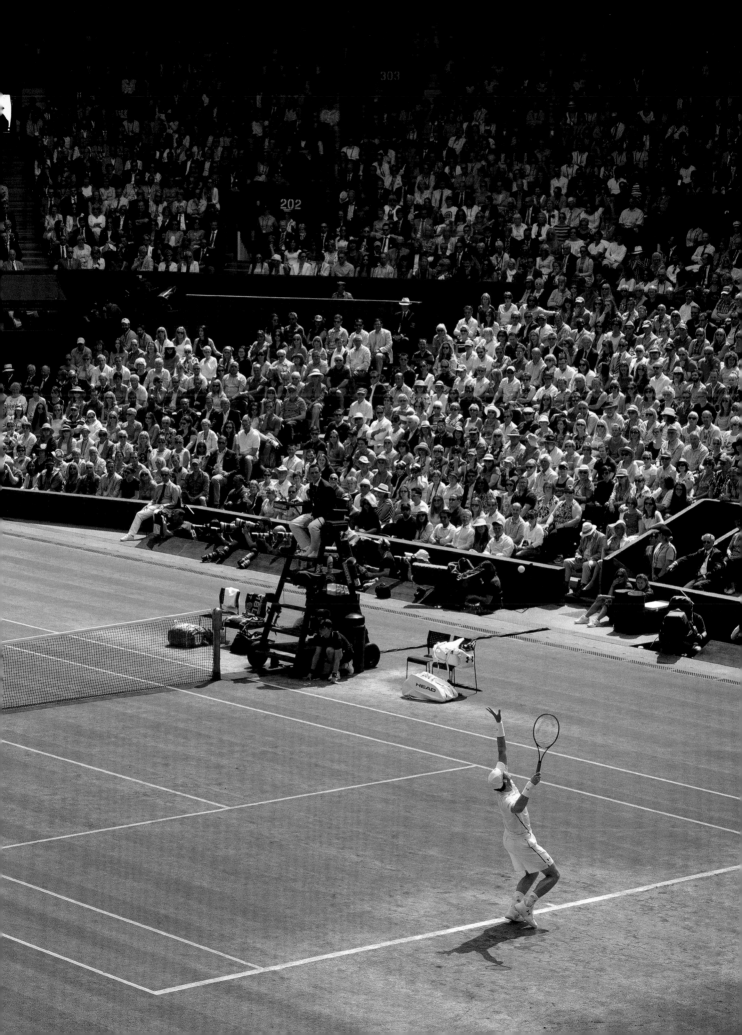

From 'The Hill' to the Royal Box, the support for Britain's tennis superstar was loud and proud

the equal second fastest in the history of The Championships – at 4-4 in the second set. Murray's backhand return was so good that he was able to punish Raonic's subsequent forehand with a beautifully timed backhand cross-court pass winner.

Raonic had averaged 25 aces per match in the previous six rounds but could manage only eight against Murray, who forced seven break points to the Canadian's two. Murray converted only one of them – Raonic converted neither of his, which both came in the third set – but, crucially, won five out of nine points against serve in the two tie-breaks, whereas his opponent won only one out of 10. Murray, who made only 12 unforced errors to Raonic's 29, was effective when he came to the net, though it was generally Raonic who came charging forward, only to be beaten on a regular basis by thunderous passing shots or clever changes of pace.

On a beautiful summer's afternoon the regular rain stoppages of the first week felt like a distant memory as the guests took their seats in the Royal Box. The Duke and Duchess of Cambridge were joined by, among others, several other members of the Royal Family, the soon-to-be-departing Prime Minister David Cameron, the actors Benedict Cumberbatch and Hugh Grant, and a number of former Wimbledon champions, including Boris Becker, Stefan Edberg, Bjorn Borg, Roy Emerson, Chris Evert, Manuel Santana and Stan Smith.

After the warm-up it was clear who was the more nervous player on the court. While an almost casual Murray took his time rising from his chair and then tied up his shoelaces on the way to the back of the court, Raonic was jumping up and down like a jack-in-the-box, clearly anxious to get the match under way.

The battle lines were drawn in only the third game as Murray attacked Raonic's serve on his first break point. The Canadian hung on until Murray converted his third break point at 3-3 when his crunching forehand forced a volley error. Having served out for the first set, Murray had four more break points in the second but could not take any of them. The world No.2 won the first three points of the tie-break, cracked a forehand winner after returning a Raonic smash at 1-3 and eventually won it 7-3.

Previous pages: After a fortnight punctuated by stoppages for rain, the sun shone on the final day and Centre Court was bathed in glorious sunshine for much of the Gentlemen's Singles Final

Below: With the cheers ringing in his ears, Murray delivered a clinical display of ruthless tennis which battered Raonic into submission

Right: Having become the first Canadian man to reach a Grand Slam singles final, Milos Raonic could hold his head up high having done his country proud

Below: After shedding a few tears, the 2016 Wimbledon Gentlemen's Singles champion gathered himself together for the trophy presentation

Far right: Murray seemed more relaxed than in 2013 and later admitted he had been able to enjoy the moment a little more, second time around

Right: All England Club Chairman Philip Brook congratulates the new champion in front of the Centre Court honours board, already updated with '2016 A. Murray'

Far right: Go on, give us a kiss! Murray shows the ecstatic fans who have gathered below the Centre Court balcony what winning Wimbledon means to him

After more than two hours of play, Raonic had his only break points of the match at 2-2 in the third set but could take neither of them. Murray bellowed out a roar of celebration after holding serve and the set eventually went to another tie-break. Raonic immediately went down two mini-breaks under attack from Murray, who eventually converted his second match point to secure his 6-4, 7-6(3), 7-6(2) victory when the Canadian put a backhand in the net. The Scot had largely kept his emotions in check until that moment but as he sat in his chair before the presentation ceremony the tears flowed.

"I'm just really proud that I managed to do it again after a lot of tough losses in the latter stages of the Slams over the last couple of years," Murray said, adding that becoming a father earlier in the year had given him plenty of extra motivation. Raonic said he had done the best he could but added: "This one is going to sting so I'm going to make sure that as long as these courts are green I'll do everything I can to be back here for another chance."

When Murray ended Britain's 77-year wait for a Gentlemen's Singles champion at Wimbledon three years earlier, after a nerve-shredding finale against Djokovic, his overwhelming emotion had been one of relief. This time he said he was determined to enjoy the victory.

"The last time it was such a big thing for a British man to win Wimbledon because it had been so long," he said. "I was so relieved that I'd done that. It was a question I'd been asked so many times over the course of my career. It's something you start to think about and put more and more pressure on yourself to do it. I want to spend this time with my family, my closest friends and the people that I work with. That's who I want to be around right now. I'll make sure I spend a lot of time with them over the next couple of days."

The celebrations began when a large group of Murray's family, friends and colleagues attended that evening's Champions' Dinner in London's historic Guildhall and continued on into the night.

The headlines in Monday's newspapers were an indication of what Murray's victory meant to his country. It had been a great sporting weekend, with Portugal's footballers winning the European Championship and Lewis Hamilton winning the British Grand Prix, but the *Daily Telegraph*, reflecting on the fact that the referendum vote had divided a country that had also been "sodden by summer rain", gave the top half of its front page to a large photograph of Murray holding the Wimbledon trophy and a headline that read: "At last, something for the whole nation to cheer".

After Murray's triumph Heather Watson had continued a remarkable day for British tennis when she partnered Finland's Henri Kontinen to victory over Colombia's Robert Farah and Germany's Anna-Lena Groenefeld 7-6(5), 6-4 in the final of the Mixed Doubles. Watson became the first British Mixed Doubles champion at The Championships since Jamie Murray in 2007 and the first British female champion in any event since Jo Durie partnered Jeremy Bates to victory in 1987.

On a wonderful day for British tennis, Heather Watson was overcome with joy at winning the Mixed Doubles Final with partner Henri Kontinen of Finland

Watson and Kontinen were unseeded and had never played together before the tournament but performed well from the start, although they were handed free passages through the first two rounds after their opponents withdrew. Kontinen described Wimbledon as "a special place to win" and "the tournament that every player has in their mind", while Watson said she would remember her victory for ever. "It's been a dream of mine since I was a little girl to be a Grand Slam champion," she said. "I would take anything – singles, doubles, mixed doubles. I've got one of those now."

Watson, whose first week of the Fortnight had been less than memorable after she lost in the first round of the singles and was handed the second biggest fine in Wimbledon history of $12,000 for thumping the court with her racket, said she hoped her doubles success would help her singles game. "I think it's something I can use moving forward," she said. "I always try to play doubles as much as I can because I really enjoy it. With my game style in singles, I'm always trying to come to the net more. I felt like my volleys have really improved this week."

The day had begun with another British victory in the inaugural Gentlemen's Wheelchair Singles event as Gordon Reid beat Sweden's Stefan Olsson 6-1, 6-4. Reid, who had also won the doubles title the previous day alongside his fellow Briton Alfie Hewett, was cheered on by a packed crowd on Court 17, including many who were wearing Alice bands in recognition of the Scot's trademark. Reid said afterwards: "A Wimbledon title was always going to be unbelievable, but to be the first ever to win the singles event, I'm never going to forget that."

It was also a memorable day for Canada, despite Raonic's defeat. The world No.9's compatriot, Denis Shapovalov, won the boys' title after recovering from a slow start to beat Australia's Alex De Minaur 4-6, 6-1, 6-3 in the final. "In the second set I found my confidence," Shapovalov said afterwards. "I told myself: 'I'm going to go for it. I don't care if I miss. I'm going to go for my shots'."

There had been occasions in the rain-battered first week when we had wondered whether The Championships would ever finish on schedule, but by the time the gates were shut on the final Sunday the competition was complete. It had been a memorable tournament, full of thrilling matches, remarkable feats and relentless endeavour. The only sadness was that we would have to wait 50 more weeks to enjoy the next set of indelible memories.

The Champion's Fall (nearly!)

Unlike the final earlier in the day, in which he didn't put a foot wrong, Andy Murray narrowly avoided a tumble at the Wimbledon Champions' Ball

● **Andy Murray's mum, Judy, may have once graced** *Strictly Come Dancing* but her lad, Wimbledon champion once again, sidestepped the chance to dance with Ladies' Singles champion Serena Williams at the Champions' Ball. He may not have tripped the light fantastic – but he did trip.

"It's a nice thing to do but it never really happened this year, and I was just lucky to leave the stage in one piece," Murray said.

"When Serena and I were coming off the stage together a few people were shouting 'dance, dance!' – and I got distracted and literally fell down the stairs. I had dress shoes on with slippy soles and things almost got a bit ugly."

● **Gordon Reid revealed the preparations** for his historic inaugural Gentlemen's Wheelchair Singles triumph had been far from ideal thanks to some partying tennis folk.

"I was staying at the National Tennis Centre the last two weeks. There was a party on last night that went on until one in the morning and I ended up moving hotels at 10 on the eve of the final to escape the noise. It wasn't ideal," recalled the Scot.

Fortunately, an official helped quickly sort out a hotel for him 10 minutes' drive down the road and, though he had "a bit of restless sleep", he was still just about fresh enough to win his big match against Stefan Olsson.

Never mind the tennis, Benedict Cumberbatch revealed to Andy Murray that there will be a new series of Sherlock!

● **As he soaked up all the congratulations** just minutes after collecting the trophy, Murray, prize tucked under his arm, bumped into the actor Benedict Cumberbatch – and it was hard to tell which man was the more star-struck.

Murray didn't sound bothered about talking tennis, telling Cumberbatch what a big fan he was and asking him what he was up to. When told he was filming a new series of *Sherlock*, Murray gave a fist pump and enthused, "Yes!"

You could have sworn at that moment he'd forgotten that he'd just won Wimbledon.

● **It seemed fitting that on the last day of The Championships**, we should get one more reminder of the man who so illuminated proceedings on the first. Remember Marcus Willis?

A poll by the BBC voted Willis' brilliant running two-fisted backhand lob, delivered after he'd slipped and had to scramble back into the rally against Roger Federer on Centre Court, as the shot of The Championships – the perfect ending to his fairytale.

The morning after the day before

On the morning following his triumph over Milos Raonic, and after a late night during which he admitted he had indulged in "a few drinks", Andy Murray returned to a somewhat quieter and more sedate Wimbledon.

Following the traditional 'day after' press conference at which he was relaxed and amenable as always – talking in particular about the new focus the arrival of his baby daughter, Sophia, has given him – he agreed to a photocall with the

And then, having posed for numerous pictures and the now-obligatory selfies, and still clutching the trophy which it looked like he never wanted to let go of, he took the opportunity for a stroll across the hallowed turf.

It was a chance, presumably, to reflect on how moments that have taken place on that very grass have changed the course of his life, not to mention British tennis and, indeed, British sport.

Let's hope there are many more such moments.

WIMBLEDON 2016

The Gentlemen's Singles

 Andy MURRAY

The Ladies' Singles

 Serena WILLIAMS

The Gentlemen's Doubles

 Pierre-Hugues HERBERT **Nicolas MAHUT**

The Ladies' Doubles

 Serena WILLIAMS **Venus WILLIAMS**

The Mixed Doubles

 Henri KONTINEN **Heather WATSON**

THE CHAMPIONS

The Boys' Singles

Denis SHAPOVALOV

The Girls' Singles

Anastasia POTAPOVA

The Boys' Doubles

**Kenneth RAISMA
Stefanos TSITSIPAS**

The Girls' Doubles

**Usue Maitane ARCONADA
Claire LIU**

The Gentlemen's Invitation Doubles

**Greg RUSEDSKI
Fabrice SANTORO**

The Ladies' Invitation Doubles

**Martina NAVRATILOVA
Selima SFAR**

The Gentlemen's Senior Invitation Doubles

**Todd WOODBRIDGE
Mark WOODFORDE**

The Gentlemen's Wheelchair Singles

Gordon REID

The Ladies' Wheelchair Singles

Jiske GRIFFIOEN

The Gentlemen's Wheelchair Doubles

**Alfie HEWETT
Gordon REID**

The Ladies' Wheelchair Doubles

**Yui KAMIJI
Jordanne WHILEY**

EVENT 1 – THE GENTLEMEN'S SINGLES CHAMPIONSHIP 2016
Holder: NOVAK DJOKOVIC (SRB)

The Champion will become the holder, for the year only, of the CHALLENGE CUP presented by The All England Lawn Tennis and Croquet Club in 1887. The Champion will receive a silver three-quarter size replica of the Challenge Cup.
A Silver Salver will be presented to the Runner-up and a Bronze Medal to each defeated semi-finalist. The matches will be the best of five sets.

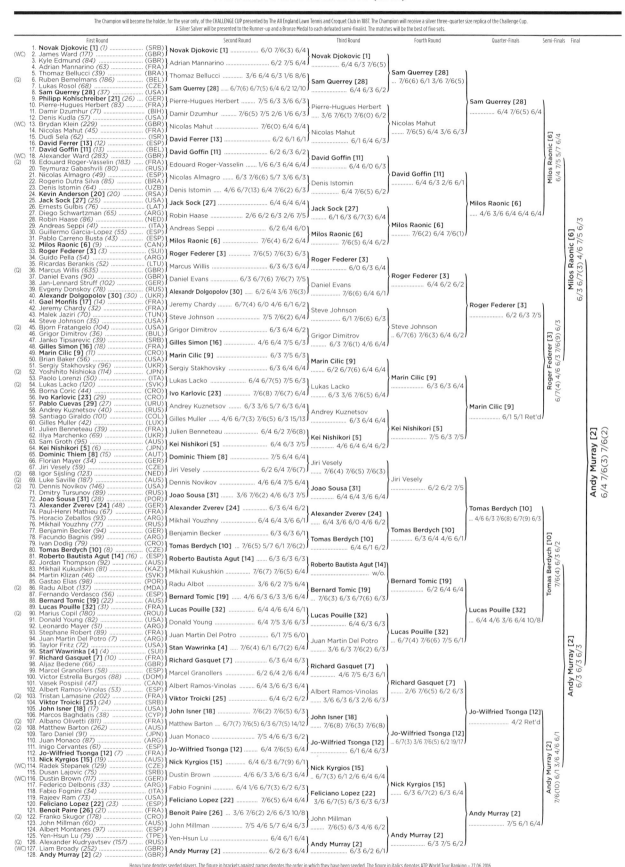

Heavy type denotes seeded players. The figure in brackets against names denotes the order in which they have been seeded. The figure in italics denotes ATP World Tour Ranking – 27.06.2016
(WC) = Wild cards. (Q) = Qualifiers. (LL) = Lucky loser.

EVENT 2 – THE GENTLEMEN'S DOUBLES CHAMPIONSHIP 2016
Holders: JEAN-JULIEN ROJER (NED) & HORIA TECAU (ROU)

The Champions will become the holders, for the year only, of the CHALLENGE CUPS presented by the OXFORD UNIVERSITY LAWN TENNIS CLUB in 1884 and the late SIR HERBERT WILBERFORCE in 1937.
The Champions will receive a silver three-quarter size replica of the Challenge Cup. A Silver Salver will be presented to each of the Runners-up, and a Bronze Medal to each defeated semi-finalist. The matches are the best of five sets.

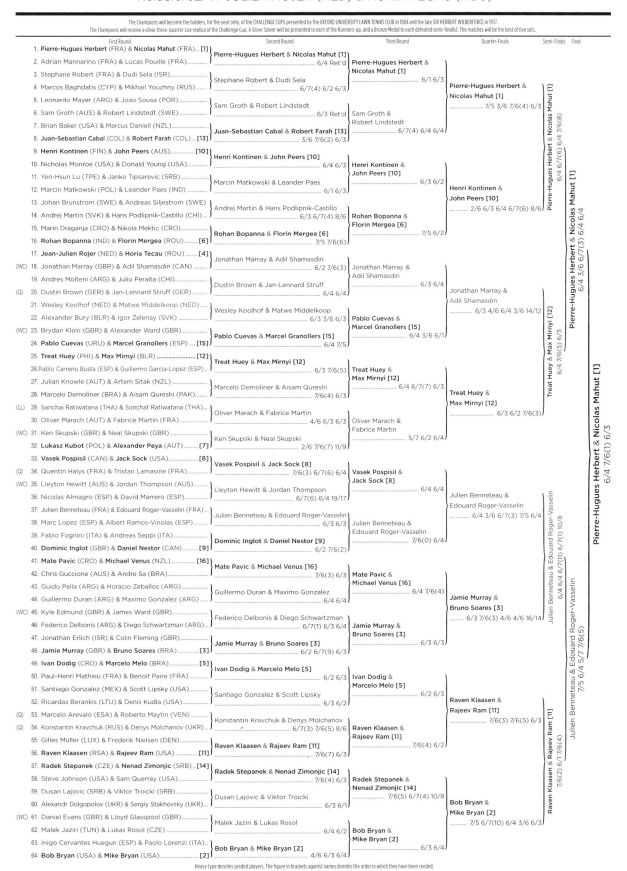

First Round	Second Round	Third Round	Quarter-Finals	Semi-Finals	Final

1. Pierre-Hugues Herbert (FRA) & Nicolas Mahut (FRA)... [1]
2. Adrian Mannarino (FRA) & Lucas Pouille (FRA)
3. Stephane Robert (FRA) & Dudi Sela (ISR)
4. Marcos Baghdatis (CYP) & Mikhail Youzhny (RUS)
5. Leonardo Mayer (ARG) & Joao Sousa (POR)
6. Sam Groth (AUS) & Robert Lindstedt (SWE)
7. Brian Baker (USA) & Marcus Daniell (NZL)
8. Juan-Sebastian Cabal (COL) & Robert Farah (COL) [13]
9. Henri Kontinen (FIN) & John Peers (AUS) [10]
10. Nicholas Monroe (USA) & Donald Young (USA)
11. Yen-Hsun Lu (TPE) & Janko Tipsarevic (SRB)
12. Marcin Matkowski (POL) & Leander Paes (IND)
13. Johan Brunstrom (SWE) & Andreas Siljestrom (SWE)
14. Andrej Martin (SVK) & Hans Podlipnik-Castillo (CHI)
15. Marin Draganja (CRO) & Nikola Mektic (CRO)
16. Rohan Bopanna (IND) & Florin Mergea (ROU) [6]
17. Jean-Julien Rojer (NED) & Horia Tecau (ROU) [4]
(WC) 18. Jonathan Marray (GBR) & Adil Shamasdin (CAN)
19. Andres Molteni (ARG) & Julio Peralta (CHI)
(Q) 20. Dustin Brown (GER) & Jan-Lennard Struff (GER)
21. Wesley Koolhof (NED) & Matwe Middelkoop (NED)
22. Alexander Bury (BLR) & Igor Zelenay (SVK)
(WC) 23. Brydan Klein (GBR) & Alexander Ward (GBR)
24. Pablo Cuevas (URU) & Marcel Granollers (ESP) [15]
25. Treat Huey (PHI) & Max Mirnyi (BLR) [12]
26. Pablo Carreno Busta (ESP) & Guillermo Garcia-Lopez (ESP)
27. Julian Knowle (AUT) & Artem Sitak (NZL)
28. Marcelo Demoliner (BRA) & Aisam Qureshi (PAK)
(LL) 29. Sanchai Ratiwatana (THA) & Sonchat Ratiwatana (THA)
30. Oliver Marach (AUT) & Fabrice Martin (FRA)
(WC) 31. Ken Skupski (GBR) & Neal Skupski (GBR)
32. Lukasz Kubot (POL) & Alexander Peya (AUT) [7]
33. Vasek Pospisil (CAN) & Jack Sock (USA) [8]
(Q) 34. Quentin Halys (FRA) & Tristan Lamasine (FRA)
(WC) 35. Lleyton Hewitt (AUS) & Jordan Thompson (AUS)
36. Nicolas Almagro (ESP) & David Marrero (ESP)
37. Julien Benneteau (FRA) & Edouard Roger-Vasselin (FRA)
38. Marc Lopez (ESP) & Albert Ramos-Vinolas (ESP)
39. Fabio Fognini (ITA) & Andreas Seppi (ITA)
40. Dominic Inglot (GBR) & Daniel Nestor (CAN) [9]
41. Mate Pavic (CRO) & Michael Venus (NZL) [16]
42. Chris Guccione (AUS) & Andre Sa (BRA)
43. Guido Pella (ARG) & Horacio Zeballos (ARG)
44. Guillermo Duran (ARG) & Maximo Gonzalez (ARG)
(WC) 45. Kyle Edmund (GBR) & James Ward (GBR)
46. Federico Delbonis (ARG) & Diego Schwartzman (ARG)
47. Jonathan Erlich (ISR) & Colin Fleming (GBR)
48. Jamie Murray (GBR) & Bruno Soares (BRA) [3]
49. Ivan Dodig (CRO) & Marcelo Melo (BRA) [5]
50. Paul-Henri Mathieu (FRA) & Benoit Paire (FRA)
51. Santiago Gonzalez (MEX) & Scott Lipsky (USA)
52. Ricardas Berankis (LTU) & Denis Kudla (USA)
(Q) 53. Marcelo Arevalo (ESA) & Roberto Maytin (VEN)
(Q) 54. Konstantin Kravchuk (RUS) & Denys Molchanov (UKR)
55. Gilles Muller (LUX) & Frederik Nielsen (DEN)
56. Raven Klaasen (RSA) & Rajeev Ram (USA) [11]
57. Radek Stepanek (CZE) & Nenad Zimonjic (SRB) [14]
58. Steve Johnson (USA) & Sam Querrey (USA)
59. Dusan Lajovic (SRB) & Viktor Troicki (SRB)
60. Alexandr Dolgopolov (UKR) & Sergiy Stakhovsky (UKR)
(WC) 61. Daniel Evans (GBR) & Lloyd Glasspool (GBR)
62. Malek Jaziri (TUN) & Lukas Rosol (CZE)
63. Inigo Cervantes Huegun (ESP) & Paolo Lorenzi (ITA)
64. Bob Bryan (USA) & Mike Bryan (USA) [2]

Second Round
Pierre-Hugues Herbert & Nicolas Mahut [1] ...... 6/4 Ret'd
Stephane Robert & Dudi Sela ...... 6/7(4) 6/2 6/3
Sam Groth & Robert Lindstedt ...... 6/3 Ret'd
Juan-Sebastian Cabal & Robert Farah [13] ...... 3/6 7/6(2) 6/3
Henri Kontinen & John Peers [10] 6/4 6/3
Marcin Matkowski & Leander Paes 6/1 6/3
Andrej Martin & Hans Podlipnik-Castillo ...... 6/3 6/7(4) 8/6
Rohan Bopanna & Florin Mergea [6] ...... 7/5 7/6(6)
Jonathan Marray & Adil Shamasdin ...... 6/2 7/6(3)
Dustin Brown & Jan-Lennard Struff 6/4 6/4
Wesley Koolhof & Matwe Middelkoop 6/3 3/6 6/3
Pablo Cuevas & Marcel Granollers [15] 6/4 7/5
Treat Huey & Max Mirnyi [12] ...... 6/3 7/6(5)
Marcelo Demoliner & Aisam Qureshi ...... 7/6(4) 6/3
Oliver Marach & Fabrice Martin 4/6 6/3 6/3
Ken Skupski & Neal Skupski ...... 2/6 7/6(7) 11/9
Vasek Pospisil & Jack Sock [8] ...... 7/6(3) 6/7(6) 6/4
Lleyton Hewitt & Jordan Thompson ...... 6/7(6) 6/4 19/17
Julien Benneteau & Edouard Roger-Vasselin 6/3 6/3
Dominic Inglot & Daniel Nestor [9] ...... 6/2 7/6(2)
Mate Pavic & Michael Venus [16] ...... 7/6(3) 6/3
Guillermo Duran & Maximo Gonzalez 6/4 6/4
Federico Delbonis & Diego Schwartzman ...... 6/7(1) 6/3 6/4
Jamie Murray & Bruno Soares [3] ...... 6/2 7/6(9) 6/3
Ivan Dodig & Marcelo Melo [5] 6/2 6/3
Santiago Gonzalez & Scott Lipsky 6/3 6/2
Konstantin Kravchuk & Denys Molchanov ...... 6/7(3) 7/6(5) 8/6
Raven Klaasen & Rajeev Ram [11] ...... 7/6(7) 6/3
Radek Stepanek & Nenad Zimonjic [14] ...... 7/6(2) 7/6(4) 6/3
Dusan Lajovic & Viktor Troicki 6/3 6/1
Malek Jaziri & Lukas Rosol 6/4 6/2
Bob Bryan & Mike Bryan [2] 4/6 6/3 6/4

Third Round
Pierre-Hugues Herbert & Nicolas Mahut [1] 6/1 6/3
Sam Groth & Robert Lindstedt ...... 6/7(4) 6/4 6/4
Henri Kontinen & John Peers [10] 6/3 6/2
Rohan Bopanna & Florin Mergea [6] 7/5 6/2
Jonathan Marray & Adil Shamasdin 6/3 6/4
Pablo Cuevas & Marcel Granollers [15] 6/4 3/6 6/1
Treat Huey & Max Mirnyi [12] ...... 6/4 6/7(7) 6/3
Oliver Marach & Fabrice Martin 5/7 6/2 6/4
Vasek Pospisil & Jack Sock [8] 6/4 6/4
Julien Benneteau & Edouard Roger-Vasselin ...... 7/6(0) 6/4
Mate Pavic & Michael Venus [16] ...... 6/4 7/6(4)
Jamie Murray & Bruno Soares [3] 6/3 6/3
Ivan Dodig & Marcelo Melo [5] 6/2 6/3
Raven Klaasen & Rajeev Ram [11] ...... 7/6(4) 6/2
Radek Stepanek & Nenad Zimonjic [14] ...... 7/6(5) 6/7(4) 10/8
Bob Bryan & Mike Bryan [2] 6/3 6/4

Quarter-Finals
Pierre-Hugues Herbert & Nicolas Mahut [1] ...... 7/5 3/6 7/6(4) 6/3
Henri Kontinen & John Peers [10] ...... 2/6 6/3 6/4 6/7(6) 8/6
Jonathan Marray & Adil Shamasdin 6/3 4/6 6/4 3/6 14/12
Treat Huey & Max Mirnyi [12] ...... 6/3 6/2 7/6(3)
Julien Benneteau & Edouard Roger-Vasselin ...... 6/4 3/6 6/7(3) 7/5 6/4
Jamie Murray & Bruno Soares [3] ...... 6/3 7/6(3) 4/6 4/6 16/14
Raven Klaasen & Rajeev Ram [11] ...... 7/6(3) 7/6(5) 6/3
Bob Bryan & Mike Bryan [2] ...... 7/5 6/7(10) 6/4 3/6 6/3

Semi-Finals
Pierre-Hugues Herbert & Nicolas Mahut [1] ...... 6/4 6/7(6) 6/7(3) 6/4 6/4
Treat Huey & Max Mirnyi [12] ...... 6/4 7/6(5) 6/3
Pierre-Hugues Herbert & Nicolas Mahut [1] ...... 6/4 3/6 6/7(3) 6/4 6/4
Julien Benneteau & Edouard Roger-Vasselin ...... 6/4 6/4 6/7(1) 6/7(1) 10/8
Raven Klaasen & Rajeev Ram [11] ...... 7/6(2) 6/1 7/6(4)
Julien Benneteau & Edouard Roger-Vasselin ...... 7/5 6/4 5/7 7/6(5)

Final
Pierre-Hugues Herbert & Nicolas Mahut [1] ...... 6/4 7/6(1) 6/3

Heavy type denotes seeded players. The figure in brackets against names denotes the order in which they have been seeded.
(WC) = Wild cards. (Q) = Qualifiers. (LL) = Lucky losers.

EVENT 3 – THE LADIES' SINGLES CHAMPIONSHIP 2016
Holder: SERENA WILLIAMS (USA)

The Champion will become the holder, for the year only, of the CHALLENGE TROPHY presented by The All England Lawn Tennis and Croquet Club in 1886. The Champion will receive a silver three-quarter size replica of the Challenge Trophy.
A Silver Salver will be presented to the Runner-up and a Bronze Medal to each defeated semi-finalist. The matches will be the best of three sets.

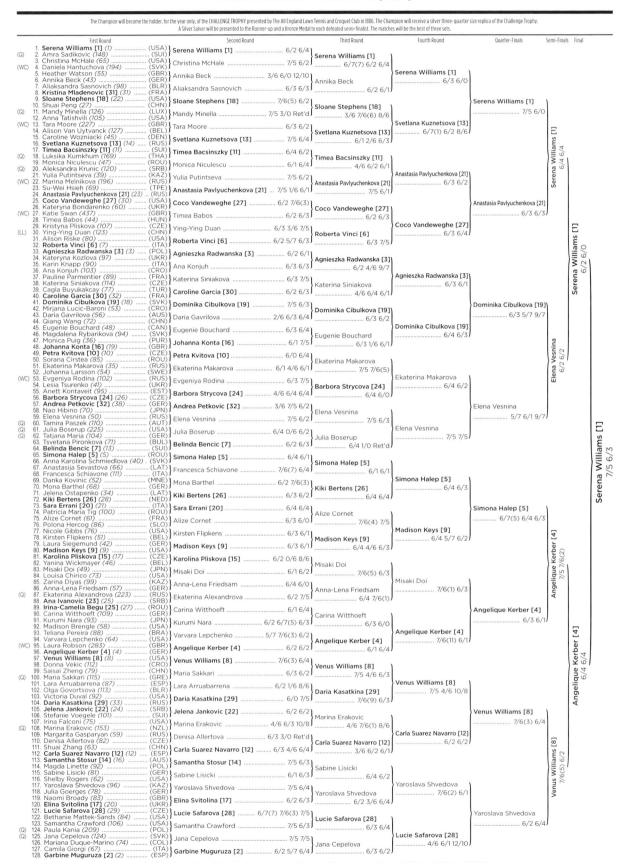

Columns: First Round — Second Round — Third Round — Fourth Round — Quarter-Finals — Semi-Finals — Final

First Round

1. **Serena Williams [1]** (1) .... (USA)
(Q) 2. Amra Sadikovic (148) .... (SUI)
3. Christina McHale (65) .... (USA)
(WC) 4. Daniela Hantuchova (194) .... (SVK)
5. Heather Watson (55) .... (GBR)
6. Annika Beck (43) .... (GER)
7. Aliaksandra Sasnovich (98) .... (BLR)
8. **Kristina Mladenovic [31]** (31) .... (FRA)
9. **Sloane Stephens [18]** (22) .... (USA)
10. Shuai Peng (27) .... (CHN)
(Q) 11. Mandy Minella (126) .... (LUX)
12. Anna Tatishvili (105) .... (USA)
(WC) 13. Tara Moore (227) .... (GBR)
14. Alison Van Uytvanck (127) .... (BEL)
15. Caroline Wozniacki (45) .... (DEN)
16. **Svetlana Kuznetsova [13]** (14) .... (RUS)
17. **Timea Bacsinszky [11]** (11) .... (SUI)
(Q) 18. Luksika Kumkhum (169) .... (THA)
19. Monica Niculescu (47) .... (ROU)
(Q) 20. Aleksandra Krunic (120) .... (SRB)
21. Yulia Putintseva (39) .... (KAZ)
(WC) 22. Marina Melnikova (196) .... (RUS)
23. Su-Wei Hsieh (69) .... (TPE)
24. **Anastasia Pavlyuchenkova [21]** (23) .... (RUS)
25. **Coco Vandeweghe [27]** (30) .... (USA)
26. Kateryna Bondarenko (60) .... (UKR)
(WC) 27. Katie Swan (437) .... (GBR)
28. Timea Babos (44) .... (HUN)
29. Kristyna Pliskova (107) .... (CZE)
(LL) 30. Ying-Ying Duan (123) .... (CHN)
31. Alison Riske (80) .... (USA)
32. **Roberta Vinci [6]** (7) .... (ITA)
33. **Agnieszka Radwanska [3]** (3) .... (POL)
34. Kateryna Kozlova (97) .... (UKR)
35. Karin Knapp (90) .... (ITA)
36. Ana Konjuh (103) .... (CRO)
37. Pauline Parmentier (89) .... (FRA)
38. Katerina Siniakova (114) .... (CZE)
39. Cagla Buyukbakcay (77) .... (TUR)
40. **Caroline Garcia [30]** (32) .... (FRA)
41. **Dominika Cibulkova [19]** (18) .... (SVK)
42. Mirjana Lucic-Baroni (53) .... (CRO)
43. Daria Gavrilova (56) .... (AUS)
44. Qiang Wang (72) .... (CHN)
45. Eugenie Bouchard (48) .... (CAN)
46. Magdalena Rybarikova (94) .... (SVK)
47. Monica Puig (36) .... (PUR)
48. **Johanna Konta [16]** (19) .... (GBR)
49. **Petra Kvitova [10]** (10) .... (CZE)
50. Sorana Cirstea (85) .... (ROU)
51. Ekaterina Makarova (35) .... (RUS)
52. Johanna Larsson (54) .... (SWE)
(WC) 53. Evgeniya Rodina (102) .... (RUS)
54. Lesia Tsurenko (41) .... (UKR)
55. Anett Kontaveit (95) .... (EST)
56. **Barbora Strycova [24]** (26) .... (CZE)
57. **Andrea Petkovic [32]** (38) .... (GER)
58. Nao Hibino (70) .... (JPN)
59. Elena Vesnina (50) .... (RUS)
(Q) 60. Tamira Paszek (110) .... (AUT)
(Q) 61. Julia Boserup (225) .... (USA)
(Q) 62. Tatjana Maria (104) .... (GER)
63. Tsvetana Pironkova (71) .... (BUL)
64. **Belinda Bencic [7]** (13) .... (SUI)
65. **Simona Halep [5]** (5) .... (ROU)
66. Anna Karolina Schmiedlova (40) .... (SVK)
67. Anastasija Sevastova (66) .... (LAT)
68. Francesca Schiavone (111) .... (ITA)
69. Danka Kovinic (52) .... (MNE)
70. Mona Barthel (68) .... (GER)
71. Jelena Ostapenko (34) .... (LAT)
72. **Kiki Bertens [26]** (28) .... (NED)
73. **Sara Errani [20]** (21) .... (ITA)
74. Patricia Maria Tig (100) .... (ROU)
75. Alize Cornet (61) .... (FRA)
76. Polona Hercog (86) .... (SLO)
77. Nicole Gibbs (76) .... (USA)
78. Kirsten Flipkens (51) .... (BEL)
79. Laura Siegemund (42) .... (GER)
80. **Madison Keys [9]** (9) .... (USA)
81. **Karolina Pliskova [15]** (17) .... (CZE)
82. Yanina Wickmayer (46) .... (BEL)
83. Misaki Doi (49) .... (JPN)
84. Louisa Chirico (73) .... (USA)
85. Zarina Diyas (99) .... (KAZ)
86. Anna-Lena Friedsam (57) .... (GER)
(Q) 87. Ekaterina Alexandrova (223) .... (RUS)
88. **Irina-Camelia Begu [25]** (27) .... (ROU)
89. **Ana Ivanovic [23]** (25) .... (SRB)
90. Carina Witthoeft (109) .... (GER)
91. Kurumi Nara (93) .... (JPN)
92. Madison Brengle (58) .... (USA)
93. Teliana Pereira (88) .... (BRA)
94. Varvara Lepchenko (64) .... (USA)
(WC) 95. Laura Robson (283) .... (GBR)
96. **Angelique Kerber [4]** (4) .... (GER)
97. **Venus Williams [8]** (8) .... (USA)
98. Donna Vekic (112) .... (CRO)
99. Saisai Zheng (79) .... (CHN)
(Q) 100. Maria Sakkari (115) .... (GRE)
101. Lara Arruabarrena (87) .... (ESP)
102. Olga Govortsova (113) .... (BLR)
103. Victoria Duval (92) .... (USA)
104. **Daria Kasatkina [29]** (33) .... (RUS)
105. **Jelena Jankovic [22]** (24) .... (SRB)
106. Stefanie Voegele (101) .... (SUI)
107. Irina Falconi (75) .... (USA)
(Q) 108. Marina Erakovic (153) .... (NZL)
109. Margarita Gasparyan (59) .... (RUS)
110. Denisa Allertova (82) .... (CZE)
111. Shuai Zhang (63) .... (CHN)
112. **Carla Suarez Navarro [12]** (12) .... (ESP)
113. **Samantha Stosur [14]** (16) .... (AUS)
114. Magda Linette (92) .... (POL)
115. Sabine Lisicki (81) .... (GER)
116. Shelby Rogers (62) .... (USA)
117. Yaroslava Shvedova (96) .... (KAZ)
118. Julia Goerges (78) .... (GER)
119. Naomi Broady (83) .... (GBR)
120. **Elina Svitolina [17]** (20) .... (UKR)
121. **Lucie Safarova [28]** (29) .... (CZE)
122. Bethanie Mattek-Sands (84) .... (USA)
123. Samantha Crawford (106) .... (USA)
(Q) 124. Paula Kania (209) .... (POL)
(Q) 125. Jana Cepelova (124) .... (SVK)
126. Mariana Duque-Marino (74) .... (COL)
127. Camila Giorgi (67) .... (ITA)
128. **Garbine Muguruza [2]** (2) .... (ESP)

Second Round

- Serena Williams [1] — 6/2 6/4
- Christina McHale — 7/5 6/2
- Annika Beck — 3/6 6/0 12/10
- Aliaksandra Sasnovich — 6/3 6/3
- Sloane Stephens [18] — 7/6(5) 6/2
- Mandy Minella — 7/5 3/0 Ret'd
- Tara Moore — 6/3 6/2
- Svetlana Kuznetsova [13] — 7/5 6/4
- Timea Bacsinszky [11] — 6/4 6/2
- Monica Niculescu — 6/1 6/4
- Yulia Putintseva — 7/5 6/2
- Anastasia Pavlyuchenkova [21] — 7/5 1/6 6/1
- Coco Vandeweghe [27] — 6/2 7/6(3)
- Timea Babos — 6/2 6/3
- Ying-Ying Duan — 6/3 3/6 7/5
- Roberta Vinci [6] — 6/2 5/7 6/3
- Agnieszka Radwanska [3] — 6/2 6/1
- Ana Konjuh — 6/3 6/3
- Katerina Siniakova — 6/3 7/5
- Caroline Garcia [30] — 6/2 6/3
- Dominika Cibulkova [19] — 7/5 6/3
- Daria Gavrilova — 2/6 6/3 6/4
- Eugenie Bouchard — 6/3 6/4
- Johanna Konta [16] — 6/1 7/5
- Petra Kvitova [10] — 6/0 6/4
- Ekaterina Makarova — 6/1 4/6 6/1
- Evgeniya Rodina — 6/3 7/5
- Barbora Strycova [24] — 4/6 6/4 6/4
- Andrea Petkovic [32] — 3/6 7/5 6/2
- Elena Vesnina — 7/5 6/2
- Julia Boserup — 6/4 0/6 6/2
- Belinda Bencic [7] — 6/2 6/3
- Simona Halep [5] — 6/4 6/1
- Francesca Schiavone — 7/6(7) 6/4
- Mona Barthel — 6/2 7/6(3)
- Kiki Bertens [26] — 6/3 6/2
- Sara Errani [20] — 6/4 6/4
- Alize Cornet — 6/3 6/0
- Kirsten Flipkens — 6/3 6/1
- Madison Keys [9] — 6/3 6/1
- Karolina Pliskova [15] — 6/2 0/6 8/6
- Misaki Doi — 6/1 6/2
- Anna-Lena Friedsam — 6/4 6/0
- Ekaterina Alexandrova — 6/2 7/5
- Carina Witthoeft — 6/1 6/4
- Kurumi Nara — 6/2 6/7(5) 6/3
- Varvara Lepchenko — 5/7 7/6(3) 6/2
- Angelique Kerber [4] — 6/2 6/2
- Venus Williams [8] — 7/6(3) 6/4
- Maria Sakkari — 7/5 4/6 6/3
- Lara Arruabarrena — 6/2 1/6 8/6
- Daria Kasatkina [29] — 6/0 7/5
- Jelena Jankovic [22] — 7/5 6/3
- Marina Erakovic — 4/6 6/3 10/8
- Denisa Allertova — 6/3 3/0 Ret'd
- Carla Suarez Navarro [12] — 6/3 4/6 6/4
- Samantha Stosur [14] — 7/5 6/3
- Sabine Lisicki — 6/1 6/3
- Yaroslava Shvedova — 7/5 6/4
- Elina Svitolina [17] — 6/3 6/4
- Lucie Safarova [28] — 6/7(7) 7/6(3) 7/5
- Samantha Crawford — 7/5 6/3
- Jana Cepelova — 7/5 7/5
- Garbine Muguruza [2] — 6/2 5/7 6/4

Third Round

- Serena Williams [1] — 6/7(7) 6/2 6/4
- Annika Beck — 6/2 6/1
- Sloane Stephens [18] — 3/6 7/6(6) 8/6
- Svetlana Kuznetsova [13] — 6/1 2/6 6/3
- Timea Bacsinszky [11] — 4/6 6/2 6/1
- Anastasia Pavlyuchenkova [21] — 7/5 6/1
- Coco Vandeweghe [27] — 6/2 6/3
- Roberta Vinci [6] — 6/3 7/5
- Agnieszka Radwanska [3] — 6/2 4/6 9/7
- Katerina Siniakova — 4/6 6/4 6/1
- Dominika Cibulkova [19] — 6/3 6/2
- Eugenie Bouchard — 6/3 1/6 6/1
- Ekaterina Makarova — 7/5 7/6(5)
- Barbora Strycova [24] — 6/4 6/0
- Elena Vesnina — 7/5 6/3
- Julia Boserup — 6/4 1/0 Ret'd
- Simona Halep [5] — 6/1 6/1
- Kiki Bertens [26] — 6/4 6/4
- Alize Cornet — 7/6(4) 7/5
- Madison Keys [9] — 6/4 4/6 6/3
- Misaki Doi — 7/6(5) 6/3
- Anna-Lena Friedsam — 6/4 7/6(1)
- Carina Witthoeft — 6/3 6/0
- Angelique Kerber [4] — 6/1 6/4
- Venus Williams [8] — 7/5 4/6 6/3
- Daria Kasatkina [29] — 7/6(9) 6/3
- Marina Erakovic — 4/6 7/6(1) 8/6
- Carla Suarez Navarro [12] — 3/6 6/2 6/1
- Sabine Lisicki — 6/4 6/2
- Yaroslava Shvedova — 6/2 3/6 6/4
- Lucie Safarova [28] — 6/3 6/4
- Jana Cepelova — 6/3 6/2

Fourth Round

- Serena Williams [1] — 6/3 6/0
- Svetlana Kuznetsova [13] — 6/7(1) 6/2 8/6
- Anastasia Pavlyuchenkova [21] — 6/3 6/2
- Coco Vandeweghe [27] — 6/3 6/4
- Agnieszka Radwanska [3] — 6/3 6/1
- Dominika Cibulkova [19] — 6/4 6/3
- Ekaterina Makarova — 6/4 6/2
- Elena Vesnina — 7/5 7/5
- Simona Halep [5] — 6/4 6/3
- Madison Keys [9] — 6/4 5/7 6/2
- Misaki Doi — 7/6(1) 6/3
- Angelique Kerber [4] — 7/6(11) 6/1
- Venus Williams [8] — 7/5 4/6 10/8
- Carla Suarez Navarro [12] — 6/2 6/2
- Yaroslava Shvedova — 7/6(2) 6/1
- Lucie Safarova [28] — 4/6 6/1 12/10

Quarter-Finals

- Serena Williams [1] — 7/5 6/0
- Anastasia Pavlyuchenkova [21] — 6/3 6/3
- Dominika Cibulkova [19] — 6/3 5/7 9/7
- Elena Vesnina — 5/7 6/1 9/7
- Simona Halep [5] — 6/7(5) 6/4 6/3
- Angelique Kerber [4] — 6/3 6/1
- Venus Williams [8] — 7/6(3) 6/4
- Yaroslava Shvedova — 6/2 6/4

Semi-Finals

- Serena Williams [1] — 6/4 6/4
- Elena Vesnina — 6/2 6/2
- Angelique Kerber [4] — 7/5 7/6(2)
- Venus Williams [8] — 7/6(5) 6/2

Final

- Serena Williams [1] — 6/2 6/0
- Angelique Kerber [4] — 6/4 6/4

Champion: Serena Williams [1] — 7/5 6/3

Heavy type denotes seeded players. The figure in brackets against names denotes the order in which they have been seeded. The figure in italics denotes WTA Ranking – 27.06.2016.
(WC) = Wild cards. (Q) = Qualifiers. (LL) = Lucky loser.

EVENT 4 – THE LADIES' DOUBLES CHAMPIONSHIP 2016
Holders: MARTINA HINGIS (SUI) & SANIA MIRZA (IND)

The Champions will become the holders, for the year only, of the CHALLENGE CUPS presented by H.R.H. PRINCESS MARINA, DUCHESS OF KENT, the late President of The All England Lawn Tennis and Croquet Club in 1949 and The All England Lawn Tennis and Croquet Club in 2001. The Champions will receive a silver three-quarter size replica of the Challenge Cup. A Silver Salver will be presented to each of the Runners-up and a Bronze Medal to each defeated semi-finalist. The matches will be the best of three sets.

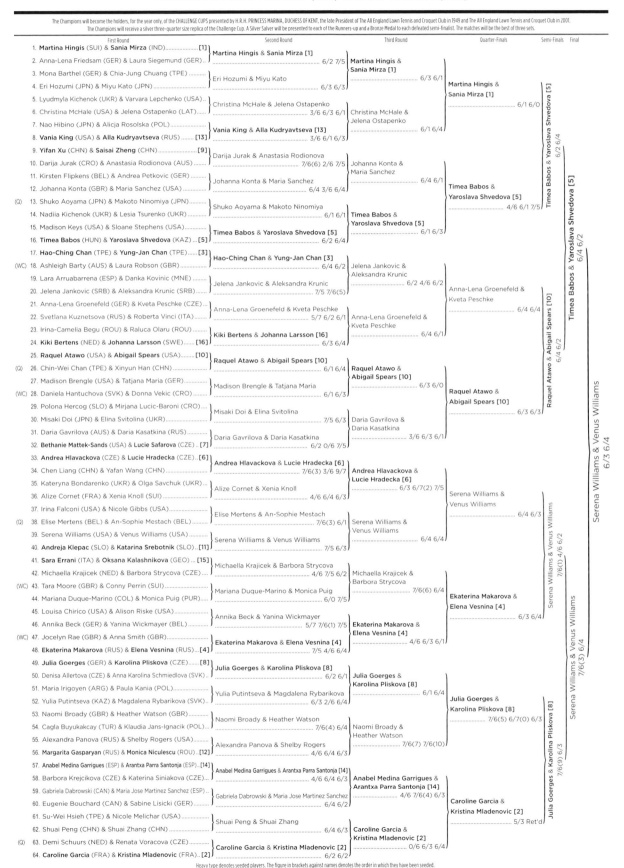

Heavy type denotes seeded players. The figure in brackets against names denotes the order in which they have been seeded.
(WC) = Wild cards. (Q) = Qualifiers. (LL) = Lucky losers.

EVENT 5 – THE MIXED DOUBLES CHAMPIONSHIP 2016
Holders: LEANDER PAES (IND) & MARTINA HINGIS (SUI)

The Champions will become the holders, for the year only, of the CHALLENGE CUPS presented by members of the family of the late Mr. S. H. SMITH in 1949 and The All England Lawn Tennis and Croquet Club in 2001.
The Champions will receive a silver three-quarter size replica of the Challenge Cup. A Silver Salver will be presented to each of the Runners-up and a Bronze Medal to each defeated semi-finalist. The matches will be the best of three sets.

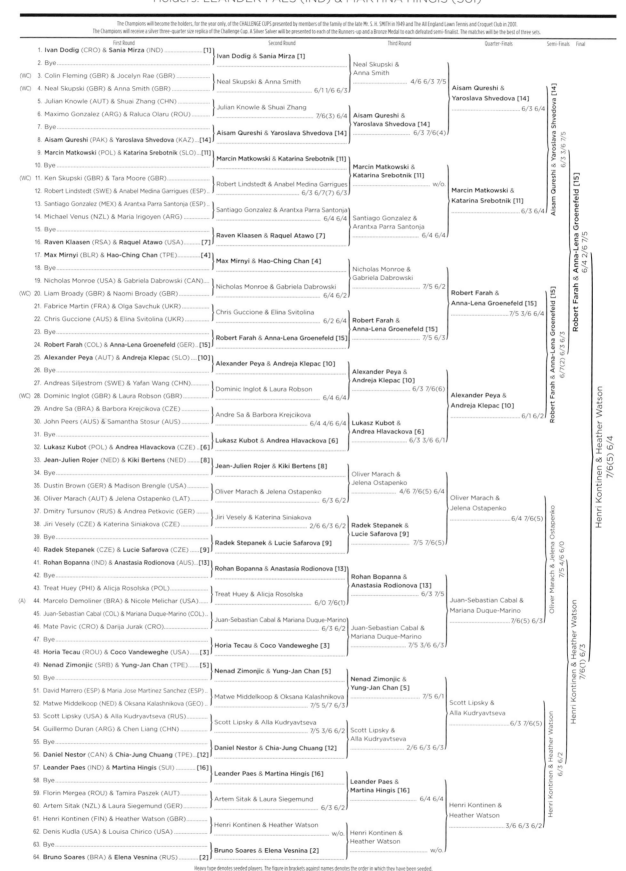

First Round	Second Round	Third Round	Quarter-Finals	Semi-Finals	Final

1. Ivan Dodig (CRO) & Sania Mirza (IND) ...... [1] — Ivan Dodig & Sania Mirza [1]
2. Bye
(WC) 3. Colin Fleming (GBR) & Jocelyn Rae (GBR) — Neal Skupski & Anna Smith 6/1 1/6 6/3
(WC) 4. Neal Skupski (GBR) & Anna Smith (GBR)
— Neal Skupski & Anna Smith 4/6 6/3 7/5
5. Julian Knowle (AUT) & Shuai Zhang (CHN) — Julian Knowle & Shuai Zhang 7/6(3) 6/4
6. Maximo Gonzalez (ARG) & Raluca Olaru (ROU)
7. Bye
8. Aisam Qureshi (PAK) & Yaroslava Shvedova (KAZ) ... [14] — Aisam Qureshi & Yaroslava Shvedova [14]
— Aisam Qureshi & Yaroslava Shvedova [14] 6/3 7/6(4)
— Aisam Qureshi & Yaroslava Shvedova [14] 6/3 6/4

9. Marcin Matkowski (POL) & Katarina Srebotnik (SLO) ... [11] — Marcin Matkowski & Katarina Srebotnik [11]
10. Bye
— Marcin Matkowski & Katarina Srebotnik [11] w/o.
(WC) 11. Ken Skupski (GBR) & Tara Moore (GBR) — Robert Lindstedt & Anabel Medina Garrigues 6/3 6/7(7) 6/3
12. Robert Lindstedt (SWE) & Anabel Medina Garrigues (ESP)
— Marcin Matkowski & Katarina Srebotnik [11] 6/3 6/4
13. Santiago Gonzalez (MEX) & Arantxa Parra Santonja (ESP) — Santiago Gonzalez & Arantxa Parra Santonja 6/4 6/4
14. Michael Venus (NZL) & Maria Irigoyen (ARG)
— Santiago Gonzalez & Arantxa Parra Santonja 6/4 6/4
15. Bye
16. Raven Klaasen (RSA) & Raquel Atawo (USA) ... [7] — Raven Klaasen & Raquel Atawo [7]

— Aisam Qureshi & Yaroslava Shvedova [14] 6/3 3/6 7/5

17. Max Mirnyi (BLR) & Hao-Ching Chan (TPE) ... [4] — Max Mirnyi & Hao-Ching Chan [4]
18. Bye
— Nicholas Monroe & Gabriela Dabrowski 7/5 6/2
19. Nicholas Monroe (USA) & Gabriela Dabrowski (CAN) — Nicholas Monroe & Gabriela Dabrowski 6/4 6/2
(WC) 20. Liam Broady (GBR) & Naomi Broady (GBR)
21. Fabrice Martin (FRA) & Olga Savchuk (UKR) — Chris Guccione & Elina Svitolina 6/2 6/4
22. Chris Guccione (AUS) & Elina Svitolina (UKR)
— Robert Farah & Anna-Lena Groenefeld [15] 7/5 6/3
23. Bye
24. Robert Farah (COL) & Anna-Lena Groenefeld (GER) ... [15] — Robert Farah & Anna-Lena Groenefeld [15]
— Robert Farah & Anna-Lena Groenefeld [15] 7/5 3/6 6/4

25. Alexander Peya (AUT) & Andreja Klepac (SLO) ... [10] — Alexander Peya & Andreja Klepac [10]
26. Bye
— Alexander Peya & Andreja Klepac [10] 6/3 7/6(6)
27. Andreas Siljestrom (SWE) & Yafan Wang (CHN) — Dominic Inglot & Laura Robson 6/4 6/4
(WC) 28. Dominic Inglot (GBR) & Laura Robson (GBR)
— Alexander Peya & Andreja Klepac [10] 6/1 6/2
29. Andre Sa (BRA) & Barbora Krejcikova (CZE) — Andre Sa & Barbora Krejcikova 6/4 4/6 6/4
30. John Peers (AUS) & Samantha Stosur (AUS)
— Lukasz Kubot & Andrea Hlavackova [6] 6/3 3/6 6/1
31. Bye
32. Lukasz Kubot (POL) & Andrea Hlavackova (CZE) ... [6] — Lukasz Kubot & Andrea Hlavackova [6]

— Robert Farah & Anna-Lena Groenefeld [15] 6/7(2) 6/3 6/3

33. Jean-Julien Rojer (NED) & Kiki Bertens (NED) ... [8] — Jean-Julien Rojer & Kiki Bertens [8]
34. Bye
— Oliver Marach & Jelena Ostapenko 4/6 7/6(5) 6/4
35. Dustin Brown (GER) & Madison Brengle (USA) — Oliver Marach & Jelena Ostapenko 6/3 6/2
36. Oliver Marach (AUT) & Jelena Ostapenko (LAT)
— Oliver Marach & Jelena Ostapenko 6/4 7/6(5)
37. Dmitry Tursunov (RUS) & Andrea Petkovic (GER) — Jiri Vesely & Katerina Siniakova 2/6 6/3 6/2
38. Jiri Vesely (CZE) & Katerina Siniakova (CZE)
— Radek Stepanek & Lucie Safarova [9] 7/5 7/6(5)
39. Bye
40. Radek Stepanek (CZE) & Lucie Safarova (CZE) ... [9] — Radek Stepanek & Lucie Safarova [9]

41. Rohan Bopanna (IND) & Anastasia Rodionova (AUS) ... [13] — Rohan Bopanna & Anastasia Rodionova [13]
42. Bye
— Rohan Bopanna & Anastasia Rodionova [13] 6/3 7/5
43. Treat Huey (PHI) & Alicja Rosolska (POL) — Treat Huey & Alicja Rosolska 6/0 7/6(1)
(A) 44. Marcelo Demoliner (BRA) & Nicole Melichar (USA)
— Juan-Sebastian Cabal & Mariana Duque-Marino 7/6(5) 6/3
45. Juan-Sebastian Cabal (COL) & Mariana Duque-Marino (COL) — Juan-Sebastian Cabal & Mariana Duque-Marino 6/3 6/2
46. Mate Pavic (CRO) & Darija Jurak (CRO)
— Juan-Sebastian Cabal & Mariana Duque-Marino 7/5 3/6 6/3
47. Bye
48. Horia Tecau (ROU) & Coco Vandeweghe (USA) ... [3] — Horia Tecau & Coco Vandeweghe [3]

— Oliver Marach & Jelena Ostapenko 7/5 4/6 6/0

49. Nenad Zimonjic (SRB) & Yung-Jan Chan (TPE) ... [5] — Nenad Zimonjic & Yung-Jan Chan [5]
50. Bye
— Nenad Zimonjic & Yung-Jan Chan [5] 7/5 6/1
51. David Marrero (ESP) & Maria Jose Martinez Sanchez (ESP) — Matwe Middelkoop & Oksana Kalashnikova 7/5 5/7 6/3
52. Matwe Middelkoop (NED) & Oksana Kalashnikova (GEO)
— Scott Lipsky & Alla Kudryavtseva 6/3 7/6(5)
53. Scott Lipsky (USA) & Alla Kudryavtseva (RUS) — Scott Lipsky & Alla Kudryavtseva 7/5 3/6 6/2
54. Guillermo Duran (ARG) & Chen Liang (CHN)
— Scott Lipsky & Alla Kudryavtseva 2/6 6/3 6/3
55. Bye
56. Daniel Nestor (CAN) & Chia-Jung Chuang (TPE) ... [12] — Daniel Nestor & Chia-Jung Chuang [12]

57. Leander Paes (IND) & Martina Hingis (SUI) ... [16] — Leander Paes & Martina Hingis [16]
58. Bye
— Leander Paes & Martina Hingis [16] 6/4 6/4
59. Florin Mergea (ROU) & Tamira Paszek (AUT) — Artem Sitak & Laura Siegemund 6/3 6/2
60. Artem Sitak (NZL) & Laura Siegemund (GER)
— Henri Kontinen & Heather Watson 3/6 6/3 6/2
61. Henri Kontinen (FIN) & Heather Watson (GBR) — Henri Kontinen & Heather Watson w/o.
62. Denis Kudla (USA) & Louisa Chirico (USA)
— Henri Kontinen & Heather Watson w/o.
63. Bye
64. Bruno Soares (BRA) & Elena Vesnina (RUS) ... [2] — Bruno Soares & Elena Vesnina [2]

— Henri Kontinen & Heather Watson 6/3 6/2 (vs Scott Lipsky & Alla Kudryavtseva)

— Juan-Sebastian Cabal & Mariana Duque-Marino (Quarter-Finals)

Semi-Finals:
Aisam Qureshi & Yaroslava Shvedova [14]
Robert Farah & Anna-Lena Groenefeld [15] 6/4 2/6 7/5

Oliver Marach & Jelena Ostapenko
Henri Kontinen & Heather Watson 7/6(1) 6/3

Final:
Robert Farah & Anna-Lena Groenefeld [15]
Henri Kontinen & Heather Watson 7/6(5) 6/4

Heavy type denotes seeded players. The figure in brackets against names denotes the order in which they have been seeded.
(A) = Alternates. (WC) = Wild cards.

EVENT 6 – THE BOYS' SINGLES CHAMPIONSHIP 2016
Holder: REILLY OPELKA (USA)

The Champion will become the holder, for the year only, of a Cup presented by The All England Lawn Tennis and Croquet Club.
The Champion will receive a three-quarter size Cup and the Runner-up will receive a Silver Salver. The matches will be the best of three sets.

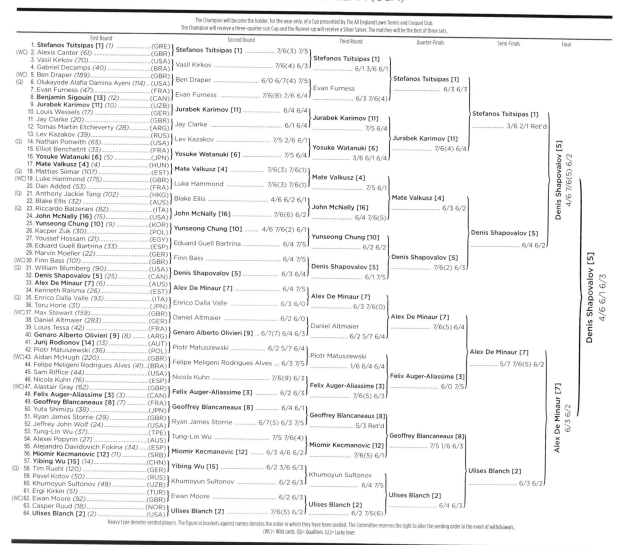

Heavy type denotes seeded players. The figure in brackets against names denotes the order in which they have been seeded. The Committee reserves the right to alter the seeding order in the event of withdrawals.
(WC)= Wild cards. (Q)= Qualifiers. (LL)= Lucky loser.

EVENT 7 – THE BOYS' DOUBLES CHAMPIONSHIP 2016
Holders: NAM HOANG LY (VIE) & SUMIT NAGAL (IND)

The Champions will become the holders, for the year only, of a Cup presented by The All England Lawn Tennis and Croquet Club.
The Champions will receive a three-quarter size Cup and the Runners-up will receive Silver Salvers. The matches will be the best of three sets.

Heavy type denotes seeded players. The figure in brackets against names denotes the order in which they have been seeded. The Committee reserves the right to alter the seeding order in the event of withdrawals.
(WC) = Wild cards. (A) = Alternates.

EVENT 8 - THE GIRLS' SINGLES CHAMPIONSHIP 2016

Holder: SOFYA ZHUK (RUS)

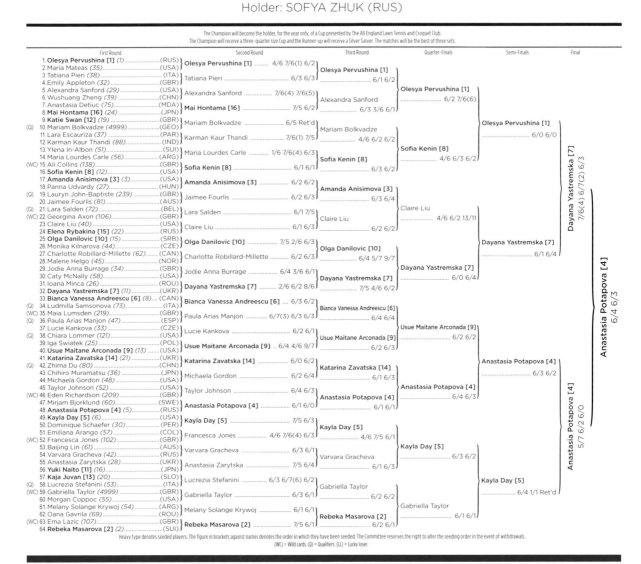

The Champion will become the holder, for the year only, of a Cup presented by The All England Lawn Tennis and Croquet Club.
The Champion will receive a three-quarter size Cup and the Runner-up will receive a Silver Salver. The matches will be the best of three sets.

First Round

1. **Olesya Pervushina [1]** *(1)* (RUS)
2. Maria Mateas *(35)* (USA)
3. Tatiana Pieri *(38)* (ITA)
4. Emily Appleton *(32)* (GBR)
5. Alexandra Sanford *(29)* (USA)
6. Wushuang Zheng *(39)* (CHN)
7. Anastasia Detiuc *(75)* (MDA)
8. **Mai Hontama [16]** *(24)* (JPN)
9. **Katie Swan [12]** *(19)* (GBR)
10. (Q) Mariam Bolkvadze *(4999)* (GEO)
11. Lara Escauriza *(37)* (PAR)
12. Karman Kaur Thandi *(88)* (IND)
13. Ylena In-Albon *(51)* (SUI)
14. Maria Lourdes Carle *(56)* (ARG)
15. (WC) Ali Collins *(138)* (GBR)
16. **Sofia Kenin [8]** *(12)* (USA)
17. **Amanda Anisimova [3]** *(3)* (USA)
18. Panna Udvardy *(27)* (HUN)
19. (Q) Lauryn John-Baptiste *(239)* (GBR)
20. Jaimee Fourlis *(81)* (AUS)
21. (Q) Lara Salden *(72)* (BEL)
22. (WC) Georgina Axon *(106)* (GBR)
23. Claire Liu *(40)* (USA)
24. **Elena Rybakina [15]** *(22)* (RUS)
25. **Olga Danilovic [10]** *(15)* (SRB)
26. Monika Kilnarova *(44)* (CZE)
27. Charlotte Robillard-Millette *(62)* (CAN)
28. Malene Helgo *(45)* (NOR)
29. Jodie Anna Burrage *(34)* (GBR)
30. Caty McNally *(58)* (USA)
31. Ioana Minca *(26)* (ROU)
32. **Dayana Yastremska [7]** *(11)* (UKR)
33. **Bianca Vanessa Andreescu [6]** *(8)* (CAN)
34. (Q) Ludmilla Samsonova *(73)* (ITA)
35. (WC) Maia Lumsden *(219)* (GBR)
36. (Q) Paula Arias Manjon *(47)* (ESP)
37. Lucie Kankova *(33)* (CZE)
38. (Q) Chiara Lommer *(121)* (USA)
39. Iga Swiatek *(25)* (POL)
40. **Usue Maitane Arconada [9]** *(13)* (USA)
41. **Katarina Zavatska [14]** *(21)* (UKR)
42. (Q) Zhima Du *(80)* (CHN)
43. Chihiro Muramatsu *(36)* (JPN)
44. Michaela Gordon *(48)* (USA)
45. Taylor Johnson *(52)* (USA)
46. (WC) Eden Richardson *(209)* (GBR)
47. Mirjam Bjorklund *(60)* (SWE)
48. **Anastasia Potapova [4]** *(5)* (RUS)
49. **Kayla Day [5]** *(6)* (USA)
50. Dominique Schaefer *(30)* (PER)
51. Emiliana Arango *(57)* (COL)
52. (WC) Francesca Jones *(102)* (GBR)
53. Baijing Lin *(61)* (AUS)
54. Varvara Gracheva *(42)* (RUS)
55. Anastasia Zarytska *(28)* (UKR)
56. **Yuki Naito [11]** *(16)* (JPN)
57. **Kaja Juvan [13]** *(20)* (SLO)
58. (Q) Lucrezia Stefanini *(53)* (ITA)
59. (WC) Gabriella Taylor *(4999)* (GBR)
60. Morgan Coppoc *(55)* (USA)
61. Melany Solange Krywoj *(54)* (ARG)
62. Oana Gavrila *(69)* (ROU)
63. (WC) Ema Lazic *(107)* (GBR)
64. **Rebeka Masarova [2]** *(2)* (SUI)

Second Round

- **Olesya Pervushina [1]** 4/6 7/6(1) 6/2
- Tatiana Pieri 6/3 6/3
- Alexandra Sanford 7/6(4) 7/6(5)
- **Mai Hontama [16]** 7/5 6/2
- Mariam Bolkvadze 6/5 Ret'd
- Karman Kaur Thandi 7/6(1) 7/5
- Maria Lourdes Carle 1/6 7/6(4) 6/3
- **Sofia Kenin [8]** 6/1 6/1
- **Amanda Anisimova [3]** 6/2 6/2
- Jaimee Fourlis 6/2 6/3
- Lara Salden 6/1 7/5
- Claire Liu 6/1 6/3
- **Olga Danilovic [10]** 7/5 2/6 6/3
- Charlotte Robillard-Millette 6/2 6/3
- Jodie Anna Burrage 6/4 3/6 6/1
- **Dayana Yastremska [7]** 2/6 6/2 8/6
- **Bianca Vanessa Andreescu [6]** 6/3 6/2
- Paula Arias Manjon 6/7(3) 6/3 6/3
- Lucie Kankova 6/2 6/1
- **Usue Maitane Arconada [9]** 6/4 4/6 9/7
- **Katarina Zavatska [14]** 6/0 6/2
- Michaela Gordon 6/2 6/4
- Taylor Johnson 6/4 6/3
- **Anastasia Potapova [4]** 6/1 6/0
- **Kayla Day [5]** 7/5 6/3
- Francesca Jones 4/6 7/6(4) 6/3
- Varvara Gracheva 6/3 6/1
- Anastasia Zarytska 7/5 6/4
- Lucrezia Stefanini 6/3 6/7(6) 6/2
- Gabriella Taylor 6/3 6/1
- Melany Solange Krywoj 6/1 6/1
- **Rebeka Masarova [2]** 7/5 6/1

Third Round

- **Olesya Pervushina [1]** 6/1 6/2
- Alexandra Sanford 6/3 3/6 6/1
- Mariam Bolkvadze 4/6 6/2 6/2
- **Sofia Kenin [8]** 6/3 6/2
- **Amanda Anisimova [3]** 6/3 6/4
- Claire Liu 6/2 6/2
- **Olga Danilovic [10]** 6/4 5/7 9/7
- **Dayana Yastremska [7]** 7/5 4/6 6/2
- **Bianca Vanessa Andreescu [6]** 6/4 6/4
- **Usue Maitane Arconada [9]** 6/2 6/3
- **Katarina Zavatska [14]** 6/1 6/3
- **Anastasia Potapova [4]** 6/1 6/1
- **Kayla Day [5]** 4/6 7/5 6/1
- Varvara Gracheva 6/1 6/3
- Gabriella Taylor 6/2 6/2
- **Rebeka Masarova [2]** 6/2 6/1

Quarter-Finals

- **Olesya Pervushina [1]** 6/2 7/6(6)
- **Sofia Kenin [8]** 4/6 6/3 6/2
- Claire Liu 4/6 6/2 13/11
- **Dayana Yastremska [7]** 6/0 6/4
- **Usue Maitane Arconada [9]** 6/2 6/2
- **Anastasia Potapova [4]** 6/4 6/3
- **Kayla Day [5]** 6/3 6/2
- Gabriella Taylor 6/1 6/1

Semi-Finals

- **Olesya Pervushina [1]** 6/0 6/0
- **Dayana Yastremska [7]** 6/1 6/4
- **Anastasia Potapova [4]** 6/3 6/2
- **Kayla Day [5]** 6/4 1/1 Ret'd

Final

- **Dayana Yastremska [7]** 7/6(4) 6/7(2) 6/3
- **Anastasia Potapova [4]** 5/7 6/2 6/0

Anastasia Potapova [4] 6/4 6/3

Heavy type denotes seeded players. The figure in brackets against names denotes the order in which they have been seeded. The Committee reserves the right to alter the seeding order in the event of withdrawals.
(WC) = Wild cards. (Q) = Qualifiers. (LL) = Lucky loser.

EVENT 9 - THE GIRLS' DOUBLES CHAMPIONSHIP 2016

Holders: DALMA GALFI (HUN) & FANNI STOLLAR (HUN)

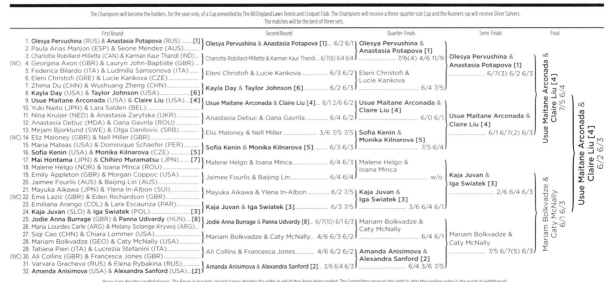

The Champions will become the holders, for the year only, of a Cup presented by The All England Lawn Tennis and Croquet Club. The Champions will receive a three-quarter size Cup and the Runners-up will receive Silver Salvers.
The matches will be the best of three sets.

First Round

1. **Olesya Pervushina** (RUS) & **Anastasia Potapova** (RUS) [1]
2. Paula Arias Manjon (ESP) & Seone Mendez (AUS)
3. Charlotte Robillard-Millette (CAN) & Karman Kaur Thandi (IND)
4. (WC) Georgina Axon (GBR) & Lauryn John-Baptiste (GBR)
5. Federica Bilardo (ITA) & Ludmilla Samsonova (ITA)
6. Eleni Christofi (GRE) & Lucie Kankova (CZE)
7. Zhima Du (CHN) & Wushuang Zheng (CHN)
8. **Kayla Day** (USA) & **Taylor Johnson** (USA) [6]
9. **Usue Maitane Arconada** (USA) & **Claire Liu** (USA) [4]
10. Yuki Naito (JPN) & Lara Salden (BEL)
11. Nina Kruijer (NED) & Anastasia Zarytska (UKR)
12. Anastasia Detiuc (MDA) & Oana Gavrila (ROU)
13. Mirjam Bjorklund (SWE) & Olga Danilovic (SRB)
14. (WC) Eliz Maloney (GBR) & Nell Miller (GBR)
15. Maria Mateas (USA) & Dominique Schaefer (PER)
16. **Sofia Kenin** (USA) & **Monika Kilnarova** (CZE) [5]
17. **Mai Hontama** (JPN) & **Chihiro Muramatsu** (JPN) [7]
18. Malene Helgo (NOR) & Ioana Minca (ROU)
19. Emily Appleton (GBR) & Morgan Coppoc (USA)
20. Jaimee Fourlis (AUS) & Baijing Lin (AUS)
21. Mayuka Aikawa (JPN) & Ylena In-Albon (SUI)
22. (WC) Ema Lazic (GBR) & Eden Richardson (GBR)
23. Emiliana Arango (COL) & Lara Escauriza (PAR)
24. **Kaja Juvan** (SLO) & **Iga Swiatek** (POL) [3]
25. **Jodie Anna Burrage** (GBR) & **Panna Udvardy** (HUN) [8]
26. Maria Lourdes Carle (ARG) & Melany Solange Krywoj (ARG)
27. Siqi Cao (CHN) & Chiara Lommer (USA)
28. Mariam Bolkvadze (GEO) & Caty McNally (USA)
29. Tatiana Pieri (ITA) & Lucrezia Stefanini (ITA)
30. (WC) Ali Collins (GBR) & Francesca Jones (GBR)
31. Varvara Gracheva (RUS) & Elena Rybakina (RUS)
32. **Amanda Anisimova** (USA) & **Alexandra Sanford** (USA) [2]

Second Round

- **Olesya Pervushina & Anastasia Potapova [1]** 6/2 6/1
- Charlotte Robillard-Millette & Karman Kaur Thandi 6/7(6) 6/4 6/4
- Eleni Christofi & Lucie Kankova 6/3 6/2
- **Kayla Day & Taylor Johnson [6]** 6/2 6/3
- **Usue Maitane Arconada & Claire Liu [4]** 6/1 2/6 6/2
- Anastasia Detiuc & Oana Gavrila 6/4 6/2
- Eliz Maloney & Nell Miller 3/6 7/5 7/5
- **Sofia Kenin & Monika Kilnarova [5]** 6/3 6/3
- Malene Helgo & Ioana Minca 6/4 6/3
- Jaimee Fourlis & Baijing Lin 6/4 6/4
- Mayuka Aikawa & Ylena In-Albon 6/2 7/5
- **Kaja Juvan & Iga Swiatek [3]** 6/3 7/5
- **Jodie Anna Burrage & Panna Udvardy [8]** 6/7(10) 6/1 6/3
- Mariam Bolkvadze & Caty McNally 4/6 6/3 6/2
- Ali Collins & Francesca Jones 4/6 6/2 6/2
- **Amanda Anisimova & Alexandra Sanford [2]** 3/6 6/4 6/3

Quarter-Finals

- **Olesya Pervushina & Anastasia Potapova [1]** 7/6(4) 4/6 11/9
- Eleni Christofi & Lucie Kankova 6/4 7/5
- **Usue Maitane Arconada & Claire Liu [4]** 6/0 6/1
- **Sofia Kenin & Monika Kilnarova [5]** 7/5 6/4
- Malene Helgo & Ioana Minca w/o.
- **Kaja Juvan & Iga Swiatek [3]** 3/6 6/4 6/1
- Mariam Bolkvadze & Caty McNally 6/4 6/1
- **Amanda Anisimova & Alexandra Sanford [2]** 6/4 3/6 7/5

Semi-Finals

- **Olesya Pervushina & Anastasia Potapova [1]** 6/7(3) 6/2 6/3
- **Usue Maitane Arconada & Claire Liu [4]** 6/1 6/7(2) 6/3
- **Kaja Juvan & Iga Swiatek [3]** 2/6 6/4 6/3
- Mariam Bolkvadze & Caty McNally 7/5 6/7(5) 6/3

Final

- **Usue Maitane Arconada & Claire Liu [4]** 7/5 6/4
- Mariam Bolkvadze & Caty McNally 6/1 6/3

Usue Maitane Arconada & Claire Liu [4] 6/2 6/3

Heavy type denotes seeded players. The figure in brackets against names denotes the order in which they have been seeded. The Committee reserves the right to alter the seeding order in the event of withdrawals.
(WC) = Wild cards. (A) = Alternates.

EVENT 10 – THE GENTLEMEN'S WHEELCHAIR SINGLES 2016

The Champion will become the holder, for the year only, of a Cup presented by The All England Lawn Tennis and Croquet Club. The Champion will receive a Silver Salver. A Silver Medal will be presented to the Runner-up.
The matches will be the best of three sets. If a match should reach one set all a 10-point tie-break will replace the third set.

First Round	Semi-final	Final
1. **Stephane Houdet [1]** *(1)* .... (FRA)	**Stephane Houdet [1]**	
2. Maikel Scheffers *(8)* .... (NED)	3/6 6/3 6/1	
3. Gustavo Fernandez *(6)* .... (ARG)	Stefan Olsson	Stefan Olsson 3/6 6/3 6/3
4. Stefan Olsson *(7)* .... (SWE)	5/7 6/2 6/2	
5. Nicolas Peifer *(3)* .... (FRA)	Gordon Reid	
6. Gordon Reid *(4)* .... (GBR)	6/3 6/4	Gordon Reid
(WC) 7. Alfie Hewett *(13)* .... (GBR)	Joachim Gerard [2]	.... 7/6(9) 6/4
8. **Joachim Gerard [2]** *(2)* .... (BEL)	6/0 6/4	

Gordon Reid 6/1 6/4

Heavy type denotes seeded players. The figure in brackets against names denotes the order in which they have been seeded. The Committee reserves the right to alter the seeding order in the event of withdrawals.
(WC) = Wild cards. (A) = Alternates.

EVENT 11 – THE GENTLEMEN'S WHEELCHAIR DOUBLES 2016
Holders: GUSTAVO FERNANDEZ (ARG) & NICOLAS PEIFER (FRA)

The Champions will become the holders, for the year only, of a Cup presented by The All England Lawn Tennis and Croquet Club. The Champions will receive a Silver Salver. A Silver Medal will be presented to each of the Runners-up.
The matches will be the best of three sets. If a match should reach one set all a 10-point tie-break will replace the third set.

First Round	Final
1. **Stephane Houdet** (FRA) & **Nicolas Peifer** (FRA) .... [1]	**Stephane Houdet & Nicolas Peifer [1]**
2. Stefan Olsson (SWE) & Maikel Scheffers (NED)	5/7 6/1 7/6(6)
3. Gustavo Fernandez (ARG) & Joachim Gerard (BEL)	**Alfie Hewett & Gordon Reid [2]**
4. **Alfie Hewett** (GBR) & **Gordon Reid** (GBR) .... [2]	6/3 6/2

Alfie Hewett & Gordon Reid [2] 4/6 6/1 7/6(6)

Heavy type denotes seeded players. The figure in brackets against names denotes the order in which they have been seeded. The Committee reserves the right to alter the seeding order in the event of withdrawals.
(WC) = Wild cards. (A) = Alternates.

EVENT 12 – THE LADIES' WHEELCHAIR SINGLES 2016

The Champion will become the holder, for the year only, of a Cup presented by The All England Lawn Tennis and Croquet Club. The Champion will receive a Silver Salver. A Silver Medal will be presented to the Runner-up.
The matches will be the best of three sets. If a match should reach one set all a 10-point tie-break will replace the third set.

First Round	Semi-final	Final
1. **Jiske Griffioen [1]** *(1)* .... (NED)	**Jiske Griffioen [1]**	
2. Sabine Ellerbrock *(6)* .... (GER)	6/4 6/4	Jiske Griffioen [1]
(WC) 3. Louise Hunt *(12)* .... (GBR)	Marjolein Buis	.... 6/7(1) 6/0 7/6(3)
4. Marjolein Buis *(5)* .... (NED)	6/2 6/0	
5. Jordanne Whiley *(3)* .... (GBR)	Jordanne Whiley	
6. Lucy Shuker *(8)* .... (GBR)	6/1 6/1	Aniek van Koot
7. Aniek van Koot *(4)* .... (NED)	Aniek van Koot	.... 7/5 6/3
8. **Yui Kamiji [2]** *(2)* .... (JPN)	2/6 7/5 6/4	

Jiske Griffioen [1] 4/6 6/0 6/4

Heavy type denotes seeded players. The figure in brackets against names denotes the order in which they have been seeded. The Committee reserves the right to alter the seeding order in the event of withdrawals.
(WC) = Wild cards. (A) = Alternates.

EVENT 13 – THE LADIES' WHEELCHAIR DOUBLES 2016
Holders: YUI KAMIJI (JPN) & JORDANNE WHILEY (GBR)

The Champions will become the holders, for the year only, of a Cup presented by The All England Lawn Tennis and Croquet Club. The Champions will receive a silver Salver. A Silver Medal will be presented to each of the Runners-up.
The matches will be the best of three sets. If a match should reach one set all a 10-point tie-break will replace the third set.

First Round	Final
1. **Yui Kamiji** (JPN) & **Jordanne Whiley** (GBR) .... [1]	**Yui Kamiji & Jordanne Whiley [1]**
2. Marjolein Buis (NED) & Louise Hunt (GBR)	6/1 6/3
3. Sabine Ellerbrock (GER) & Lucy Shuker (GBR)	**Jiske Griffioen & Aniek van Koot [2]**
4. **Jiske Griffioen** (NED) & **Aniek van Koot** (NED) .... [2]	6/1 7/6(4)

Yui Kamiji & Jordanne Whiley [1] 6/2 6/2

Heavy type denotes seeded players. The figure in brackets against names denotes the order in which they have been seeded. The Committee reserves the right to alter the seeding order in the event of withdrawals.
(WC) = Wild cards. (A) = Alternates.

181

WIMBLEDON 2016

EVENT 14 – THE GENTLEMEN'S INVITATION DOUBLES 2016
Holders: GORAN IVANISEVIC (CRO) & IVAN LJUBICIC (AUS)

The Champions will become the holders, for the year only, of a Cup presented by The All England Lawn Tennis and Croquet Club. The Champions will receive a silver three-quarter size Cup. A Silver Medal will be presented to each of the Runners-up.
The matches will be the best of three sets. If a match should reach one set all a 10-point tie-break will replace the third set.

GROUP A	Michael Chang (USA) & Mark Philippoussis (AUS)	Wayne Ferreira (RSA) & Sebastien Grosjean (FRA)	Justin Gimelstob (USA) & Ross Hutchins (GBR)	Greg Rusedski (GBR) & Fabrice Santoro (FRA)	Wins	Losses	Final
Michael Chang (USA) & Mark Philippoussis (AUS)		4/6 5/7 L	6/2 3/6 [4-10] L	3/6 4/6 L	0	3	
Wayne Ferreira (RSA) & Sebastien Grosjean (FRA)	6/4 7/5 W		3/6 6/3 [8-10] L	3/6 4/6 L	1	2	Greg Rusedski & Fabrice Santoro
Justin Gimelstob (USA) & Ross Hutchins (GBR)	2/6 6/3 [10-4] W	6/3 3/6 [10-8] W		2/6 6/3 [6-10] L	2	1	
Greg Rusedski (GBR) & Fabrice Santoro (FRA)	6/3 6/4 W	6/3 6/4 W	6/2 3/6 [10-6] W		3	0	

Greg Rusedski & Fabrice Santoro
7/5 6/1

GROUP B	Jonas Bjorkman (SWE) & Thomas Johansson (SWE)	Jamie Delgado (GBR) & Richard Krajicek (NED)	Thomas Enqvist (SWE) & Goran Ivanisevic (CRO)	Fernando Gonzalez (CHI) & Carlos Moya (ESP)	Wins	Losses	
Jonas Bjorkman (SWE) & Thomas Johansson (SWE)		3/6 6/4 [6-10] L	6/3 6/4 W	7/6(6) 2/6 [10-4] W	2	1	
Jamie Delgado (GBR) & Richard Krajicek (NED)	6/3 4/6 [10-6] W		3/6 3/6 L	2/6 6/3 [6-10] L	1	2	Jonas Bjorkman & Thomas Johansson
Thomas Enqvist (SWE) & Goran Ivanisevic (CRO)	3/6 4/6 L	6/3 6/3 W		6/7(4) 6/7(1) L	1	2	
Fernando Gonzalez (CHI) & Carlos Moya (ESP)	6/7(6) 6/2 [4-10] L	6/2 3/6 [10-6] W	7/6(4) 7/6(1) W		2	1	

This event consists of eight invited pairs divided into two groups, playing each other within their group on a 'round robin' basis. The group winner is the pair with the highest number of wins.
In the case of a tie the winning pair may be determined by head to head results or a formula based on percentage of sets/games won to those played.

EVENT 15 – THE GENTLEMEN'S SENIOR INVITATION DOUBLES 2016
Holders: JACCO ELTINGH (NED) & PAUL HAARHUIS (FRA)

The Champions will become the holders, for the year only, of a Cup presented by The All England Lawn Tennis and Croquet Club. The Champions will receive a silver half-size Cup. A Silver Medal will be presented to each of the Runners-up.
The matches will be the best of three sets. If a match should reach one set all a 10-point tie-break will replace the third set.

GROUP A	Mansour Bahrami (IRI) & Patrick McEnroe (USA)	Jeremy Bates (GBR) & Anders Jarryd (SWE)	Rick Leach (USA) & Cedric Pioline (FRA)	Todd Woodbridge (AUS) & Mark Woodforde (AUS)	Wins	Losses	Final
Mansour Bahrami (IRI) & Patrick McEnroe (USA)		3/6 3/6 L	6/4 6/3 W	7/5 2/6 [7-10] L	1	2	
Jeremy Bates (GBR) & Anders Jarryd (SWE)	6/3 6/3 W		5/7 4/6 L	3/6 2/6 L	1	2	Todd Woodbridge & Mark Woodforde
Rick Leach (USA) & Cedric Pioline (FRA)	4/6 3/6 L	7/5 6/4 W		4/6 2/6 L	1	2	
Todd Woodbridge (AUS) & Mark Woodforde (AUS)	5/7 6/2 [10-7] W	6/3 6/2 W	6/4 6/2 W		3	0	

Todd Woodbridge & Mark Woodforde
6/2 7/5

GROUP B	Jacco Eltingh (NED) & Paul Haarhuis (NED)	Sergio Casal (ESP) & Emilio Sanchez (EPS)	Henri Leconte (FRA) & Jeff Tarango (USA)	Mark Petchey (GBR) & Chris Wilkinson (GBR)	Wins	Losses	
Jacco Eltingh (NED) & Paul Haarhuis (NED)		6/3 6/4 W	6/3 7/5 W	7/6(2) 6/3 W	3	0	
Sergio Casal (ESP) & Emilio Sanchez (EPS)	3/6 4/6 L		2/6 4/6 L	5/7 2/6 L	0	3	Jacco Eltingh & Paul Haarhuis
Henri Leconte (FRA) & Jeff Tarango (USA)	3/6 5/7 L	6/2 6/4 W		3/6 3/6 L	1	2	
Mark Petchey (GBR) & Chris Wilkinson (GBR)	6/7(2) 3/6 L	7/5 6/2 W	6/3 6/3 W		2	1	

This event consists of eight invited pairs divided into two groups, playing each other within their group on a 'round robin' basis. The group winner is the pair with the highest number of wins.
In the case of a tie the winning pair may be determined by head to head results or a formula based on percentage of sets/games won to those played.

EVENT 16 – THE LADIES' INVITATION DOUBLES 2016
Holders: MAGDALENA MALEEVA (BUL) & RENNAE STUBBS (AUS)

The Champions will become the holders, for the year only, of a Cup presented by The All England Lawn Tennis and Croquet Club. The Champions will receive a silver three-quarter size Cup. A Silver Medal will be presented to each of the Runners-up.
The matches will be the best of three sets. If a match should reach one set all a 10-point tie-break will replace the third set.

GROUP A	Tracy Austin (USA) & Sandrine Testud (FRA)	Lindsay Davenport (USA) & Mary Joe Fernandez (USA)	Magdalena Maleeva (BUL) & Rennae Stubbs (AUS)	Barbara Schett (AUT) & Nathalie Tauziat (FRA)	Wins	Losses	Final
Tracy Austin (USA) & Sandrine Testud (FRA)		3/6 3/6 L	3/6 4/6 L	1/6 5/7 L	0	3	
Lindsay Davenport (USA) & Mary Joe Fernandez (USA)	6/3 6/3 W		6/4 7/5 W	6/2 6/3 W	3	0	Lindsay Davenport & Mary Joe Fernandez
Magdalena Maleeva (BUL) & Rennae Stubbs (AUS)	6/3 6/4 W	4/6 5/7 L		6/1 6/3 W	2	1	
Barbara Schett (AUT) & Nathalie Tauziat (FRA)	6/1 7/5 W	2/6 3/6 L	1/6 3/6 L		1	2	

GROUP B	Anne Keothavong (GBR) & Melanie South (GBR)	Iva Majoli (CRO) & Arantxa Sanchez Vicario (ESP)	Martina Navratilova (USA) & Selima Sfar (TUN)	Jana Novotna (CZE) & Helena Sukova (CZE)	Wins	Losses	Final
Anne Keothavong (GBR) & Melanie South (GBR)		6/4 6/2 W	1/6 3/6 L	3/6 3/6 L	1	2	
Iva Majoli (CRO) & Arantxa Sanchez Vicario (ESP)	4/6 2/6 L		4/6 1/6 L	6/2 6/4 W	1	2	Martina Navratilova & Selima Sfar
Martina Navratilova (USA) & Selima Sfar (TUN)	6/1 6/3 W	6/4 6/1 W		6/1 6/2 W	3	0	
Jana Novotna (CZE) & Helena Sukova (CZE)	6/3 6/3 W	2/6 4/6 L	1/6 2/6 L		1	2	

Winner: Martina Navratilova & Selima Sfar 7/6(5) Ret'd

This event consists of eight invited pairs divided into two groups, playing each other within their group on a 'round robin' basis. The group winner is the pair with the highest number of wins.
In the case of a tie the winning pair may be determined by head to head results or a formula based on percentage of sets/games won to those played.

COUNTRIES IN THE CHAMPIONSHIPS 2016 – ABBREVIATIONS

ARG .... Argentina	EGY .... Egypt	KOR .... South Korea	ROU .... Romania
AUS .... Australia	ESA .... El Salvador	LAT .... Latvia	RUS .... Russia
AUT .... Austria	ESP .... Spain	LTU .... Lithuania	SLO .... Slovenia
BEL .... Belgium	EST .... Estonia	LUX .... Luxembourg	SRB .... Serbia
BLR .... Belarus	FIN .... Finland	MEX .... Mexico	SVK .... Slovakia
BIH .... Bosnia-Herzegovina	FRA .... France	MDA .... Moldova	RSA .... South Africa
BRA .... Brazil	GBR .... Great Britain	MNE .... Montenegro	SUI .... Switzerland
BUL .... Bulgaria	GEO .... Georgia	NED .... Netherlands	SWE .... Sweden
CAN .... Canada	GER .... Germany	NOR .... Norway	THA .... Thailand
CHI .... Chile	GRE .... Greece	NZL .... New Zealand	TPE .... Taipei
CHN .... China	HKG .... Hong Kong	PAK .... Pakistan	TUN .... Tunisia
COL .... Colombia	HUN .... Hungary	PAR .... Paraguay	TUR .... Turkey
CRO .... Croatia	IND .... India	PER .... Peru	UKR .... Ukraine
CYP .... Cyprus	IRI .... Iran	PHI .... Philippines	URU .... Uruguay
CZE .... Czech Republic	ISR .... Israel	POL .... Poland	USA .... USA
DEN .... Denmark	ITA .... Italy	POR .... Portugal	UZB .... Uzbekistan
DOM .... Dominican Republic	JPN .... Japan	PUR .... Puerto Rico	VEN .... Venezuela
ECU .... Ecuador	KAZ .... Kazakhstan		

ROLLS OF HONOUR
GENTLEMEN'S SINGLES CHAMPIONS & RUNNERS-UP

1877 S.W.Gore *W.C.Marshall*	**1903** H.L.Doherty *F.L.Riseley*	**1933** J.H.Crawford *H.E.Vines*	**1965** R.S.Emerson *F.S.Stolle*	**1991** M.D.Stich *B.F.Becker*
1878 P.F.Hadow *S.W.Gore*	**1904** H.L.Doherty *F.L.Riseley*	**1934** F.J.Perry *J.H.Crawford*	**1966** M.M.Santana *R.D.Ralston*	**1992** A.K.Agassi *G.S.Ivanisevic*
*1879 J.T.Hartley *V.T.St.L.Goold*	**1905** H.L.Doherty *N.E.Brookes*	**1935** F.J.Perry *G.von Cramm*	**1967** J.D.Newcombe *W.P.Bungert*	**1993** P.Sampras *J.S.Courier*
1880 J.T.Hartley *H.F.Lawford*	**1906** H.L.Doherty *F.L.Riseley*	**1936** F.J.Perry *G.von Cramm*	**1968** R.G.Laver *A.D.Roche*	**1994** P.Sampras *G.S.Ivanisevic*
1881 W.C.Renshaw *J.T.Hartley*	***1907** N.E.Brookes *A.W.Gore*	***1937** J.D.Budge *G.von Cramm*	**1969** R.G.Laver *J.D.Newcombe*	**1995** P.Sampras *B.F.Becker*
1882 W.C.Renshaw *J.E.Renshaw*	***1908** A.W.Gore *H.R.Barrett*	**1938** J.D.Budge *H.W.Austin*	**1970** J.D.Newcombe *K.R.Rosewall*	**1996** R.P.S.Krajicek *M.O.Washington*
1883 W.C.Renshaw *J.E.Renshaw*	**1909** A.W.Gore *M.J.G.Ritchie*	***1939** R.L.Riggs *E.T.Cooke*	**1971** J.D.Newcombe *S.R.Smith*	**1997** P.Sampras *C.A.Pioline*
1884 W.C.Renshaw *H.F.Lawford*	**1910** A.F.Wilding *A.W.Gore*	***1946** Y.F.M.Petra *G.E.Brown*	***1972** S.R.Smith *I.Nastase*	**1998** P.Sampras *G.S.Ivanisevic*
1885 W.C.Renshaw *H.F.Lawford*	**1911** A.F.Wilding *H.R.Barrett*	**1947** J.A.Kramer *T.P.Brown*	***1973** J.Kodes *A.Metreveli*	**1999** P.Sampras *A.K.Agassi*
1886 W.C.Renshaw *H.F.Lawford*	**1912** A.F.Wilding *A.W.Gore*	***1948** R.Falkenburg *J.E.Bromwich*	**1974** J.S.Connors *K.R.Rosewall*	**2000** P.Sampras *P.M.Rafter*
*1887 H.F.Lawford *J.E.Renshaw*	**1913** A.F.Wilding *M.E.McLoughlin*	**1949** F.R.Schroeder *J.Drobny*	**1975** A.R.Ashe *J.S.Connors*	**2001** G.Ivanisevic *P.M.Rafter*
1888 J.E.Renshaw *H.F.Lawford*	**1914** N.E.Brookes *A.F.Wilding*	***1950** J.E.Patty *F.A.Sedgman*	**1976** B.R.Borg *I.Nastase*	**2002** L.G.Hewitt *D.P.Nalbandian*
1889 W.C.Renshaw *J.E.Renshaw*	**1919** G.L.Patterson *N.E.Brookes*	**1951** R.Savitt *K.B.McGregor*	**1977** B.R.Borg *J.S.Connors*	**2003** R.Federer *M.A.Philippoussis*
1890 W.J.Hamilton *W.C.Renshaw*	**1920** W.T.Tilden *G.L.Patterson*	**1952** F.A.Sedgman *J.Drobny*	**1978** B.R.Borg *J.S.Connors*	**2004** R.Federer *A.S.Roddick*
*1891 W.Baddeley *J.Pim*	**1921** W.T.Tilden *B.I.C.Norton*	***1953** E.V.Seixas *K.Nielsen*	**1979** B.R.Borg *L.R.Tanner*	**2005** R.Federer *A.S.Roddick*
1892 W.Baddeley *J.Pim*	***†1922** G.L.Patterson *R.Lycett*	**1954** J.Drobny *K.R.Rosewall*	**1980** B.Borg *J.P.McEnroe*	**2006** R.Federer *R.Nadal*
1893 J.Pim *W.Baddeley*	***1923** W.M.Johnston *F.T.Hunter*	**1955** M.A.Trabert *K.Nielsen*	**1981** J.P.McEnroe *B.R.Borg*	**2007** R.Federer *R.Nadal*
1894 J.Pim *W.Baddeley*	***1924** J.R.Borotra *J.R.Lacoste*	***1956** L.A.Hoad *K.R.Rosewall*	**1982** J.S.Connors *J.P.McEnroe*	**2008** R.Nadal *R.Federer*
*1895 W.Baddeley *W.V.Eaves*	**1925** J.R.Lacoste *J.R.Borotra*	**1957** L.A.Hoad *A.J.Cooper*	**1983** J.P.McEnroe *C.J.Lewis*	**2009** R.Federer *A.S.Roddick*
1896 H.S.Mahony *W.Baddeley*	***1926** J.R.Borotra *H.O.Kinsey*	***1958** A.J.Cooper *N.A.Fraser*	**1984** J.P.McEnroe *J.S.Connors*	**2010** R.Nadal *T.Berdych*
1897 R.F.Doherty *H.S.Mahony*	**1927** H.J.Cochet *J.R.Borotra*	***1959** A.R.Olmedo *R.G.Laver*	**1985** B.F.Becker *K.M.Curren*	**2011** N.Djokovic *R.Nadal*
1898 R.F.Doherty *H.L.Doherty*	**1928** J.R.Lacoste *H.J.Cochet*	***1960** N.A.Fraser *R.G.Laver*	**1986** B.F.Becker *I.Lendl*	**2012** R.Federer *A.B.Murray*
1899 R.F.Doherty *A.W.Gore*	***1929** H.J.Cochet *J.R.Borotra*	**1961** R.G.Laver *C.R.McKinley*	**1987** P.H.Cash *I.Lendl*	**2013** A.B.Murray *N.Djokovic*
1900 R.F.Doherty *S.H.Smith*	**1930** W.T.Tilden *W.L.Allison*	**1962** R.G.Laver *M.F.Mulligan*	**1988** S.B.Edberg *B.F.Becker*	**2014** N.Djokovic *R.Federer*
1901 A.W.Gore *R.F.Doherty*	***1931** S.B.B.Wood *F.X.Shields*	***1963** C.R.McKinley *F.S.Stolle*	**1989** B.F.Becker *S.B.Edberg*	**2015** N.Djokovic *R.Federer*
1902 H.L.Doherty *A.W.Gore*	**1932** H.E.Vines *H.W.Austin*	**1964** R.S.Emerson *F.S.Stolle*	**1990** S.B.Edberg *B.F.Becker*	**2016** A.B.Murray *M.Raonic*

For the years 1913, 1914 and 1919-1923 inclusive the above records include the 'World's Championships on Grass' granted to The Lawn Tennis Association by The International Lawn Tennis Federation. This title was then abolished and commencing in 1924 they became The Official Lawn Tennis Championships recognised by The International Lawn Tennis Federation. Prior to 1922 the holders in the Singles Events and Gentlemen's Doubles did not compete in The Championships but met the winners of these events in the Challenge Rounds.
† Challenge Round abolished: holders subsequently played through.
* The holder did not defend the title.

LADIES' SINGLES CHAMPIONS & RUNNERS-UP

1884	Miss M.E.E.Watson *Miss L.M.Watson*	1910	Mrs.R.L.Chambers *Miss P.D.H.Boothby*	*1946	Miss P.M.Betz *Miss A.L.Brough*	1972	Mrs.L.W.King *Miss E.F.Goolagong*	*1997	Miss M.Hingis *Miss J.Novotna*
1885	Miss M.E.E.Watson *Miss B.Bingley*	1911	Mrs.R.L.Chambers *Miss P.D.H.Boothby*	*1947	Miss M.E.Osborne *Miss D.J.Hart*	1973	Mrs.L.W.King *Miss C.M.Evert*	1998	Miss J.Novotna *Miss N.Tauziat*
1886	Miss B.Bingley *Miss M.E.E.Watson*	*1912	Mrs.D.T.R.Larcombe *Mrs.A.Sterry*	1948	Miss A.L.Brough *Miss D.J.Hart*	1974	Miss C.M.Evert *Mrs.O.V.Morozova*	1999	Miss L.A.Davenport *Miss S.M.Graf*
1887	Miss C.Dod *Miss B.Bingley*	*1913	Mrs.R.L.Chambers *Mrs.R.J.McNair*	1949	Miss A.L.Brough *Mrs.W.du Pont*	1975	Mrs.L.W.King *Mrs.R.A.Cawley*	2000	Miss V.E.S.Williams *Miss L.A.Davenport*
1888	Miss C.Dod *Mrs.G.W.Hillyard*	1914	Mrs.R.L.Chambers *Mrs.D.T.R.Larcombe*	1950	Miss A.L.Brough *Mrs.W.du Pont*	*1976	Miss C.M.Evert *Mrs.R.A.Cawley*	2001	Miss V.E.S.Williams *Miss J.Henin*
*1889	Mrs.G.W.Hillyard *Miss H.G.B.Rice*	1919	Miss S.R.F.Lenglen *Mrs.R.L.Chambers*	1951	Miss D.J.Hart *Miss S.J.Fry*	1977	Miss S.V.Wade *Miss B.F.Stove*	2002	Miss S.J.Williams *Miss V.E.S.Williams*
*1890	Miss H.G.B.Rice *Miss M.Jacks*	1920	Miss S.R.F.Lenglen *Mrs.R.L.Chambers*	1952	Miss M.C.Connolly *Miss A.L.Brough*	1978	Miss M.Navratilova *Miss C.M.Evert*	2003	Miss S.J.Williams *Miss V.E.S.Williams*
*1891	Miss C.Dod *Mrs.G.W.Hillyard*	1921	Miss S.R.F.Lenglen *Miss E.M.Ryan*	1953	Miss M.C.Connolly *Miss D.J.Hart*	1979	Miss M.Navratilova *Mrs.J.M.Lloyd*	2004	Miss M.Sharapova *Miss S.J.Williams*
1892	Miss C.Dod *Mrs.G.W.Hillyard*	†1922	Miss S.R.F.Lenglen *Mrs.F.I.Mallory*	1954	Miss M.C.Connolly *Miss A.L.Brough*	1980	Mrs.R.A.Cawley *Mrs.J.M.Lloyd*	2005	Miss V.E.S.Williams *Miss L.A.Davenport*
1893	Miss C.Dod *Mrs.G.W.Hillyard*	1923	Miss S.R.F.Lenglen *Miss K.McKane*	*1955	Miss A.L.Brough *Mrs.J.G.Fleitz*	*1981	Mrs.J.M.Lloyd *Miss H.Mandlikova*	2006	Miss A.Mauresmo *Mrs J.Henin-Hardenne*
*1894	Mrs.G.W.Hillyard *Miss E.L.Austin*	1924	Miss K.McKane *Miss H.N.Wills*	1956	Miss S.J.Fry *Miss A.Buxton*	1982	Miss M.Navratilova *Mrs.J.M.Lloyd*	2007	Miss V.E.S.Williams *Miss M.S.Bartoli*
*1895	Miss C.R.Cooper *Miss H.Jackson*	1925	Miss S.R.F.Lenglen *Miss J.C.Fry*	*1957	Miss A.Gibson *Miss D.R.Hard*	1983	Miss M.Navratilova *Miss A.Jaeger*	2008	Miss V.E.S.Williams *Miss S.J.Williams*
1896	Miss C.R.Cooper *Mrs.W.H.Pickering*	1926	Mrs.L.A.Godfree *Miss E.M.de Alvarez*	1958	Miss A.Gibson *Miss F.A.M.Mortimer*	1984	Miss M.Navratilova *Mrs.J.M.Lloyd*	2009	Miss S.J.Williams *Miss V.E.S.Williams*
1897	Mrs.G.W.Hillyard *Miss C.R.Cooper*	1927	Miss H.Wills *Miss E.M.de Alvarez*	*1959	Miss M.E.A.Bueno *Miss D.R.Hard*	1985	Miss M.Navratilova *Mrs.J.M.Lloyd*	2010	Miss S.J.Williams *Miss V.Zvonareva*
*1898	Miss C.R.Cooper *Miss M.L.Martin*	1928	Miss H.N.Wills *Miss E.M.de Alvarez*	1960	Miss M.E.A.Bueno *Miss S.Reynolds*	1986	Miss M.Navratilova *Miss H.Mandlikova*	2011	Miss P.Kvitova *Miss M.Sharapova*
1899	Mrs.G.W.Hillyard *Miss C.R.Cooper*	1929	Miss H.N.Wills *Miss H.H.Jacobs*	*1961	Miss F.A.M.Mortimer *Miss C.C.Truman*	1987	Miss M.Navratilova *Miss S.M.Graf*	2012	Miss S.J.Williams *Miss A.R.Radwanska*
1900	Mrs.G.W.Hillyard *Miss C.R.Cooper*	1930	Mrs.F.S.Moody *Miss E.M.Ryan*	1962	Mrs.J.R.Susman *Mrs.C.Sukova*	1988	Miss S.M.Graf *Miss M.Navratilova*	2013	Miss M.S.Bartoli *Miss S.Lisicki*
1901	Mrs.A.Sterry *Mrs.G.W.Hillyard*	*1931	Miss C.Aussem *Miss H.Krahwinkel*	*1963	Miss M.Smith *Miss B.J.Moffitt*	1989	Miss S.M.Graf *Miss M.Navratilova*	2014	Miss P.Kvitova *Miss E.C.M.Bouchard*
1902	Miss M.E.Robb *Mrs.A.Sterry*	*1932	Mrs.F.S.Moody *Miss H.H.Jacobs*	1964	Miss M.E.A.Bueno *Miss M.Smith*	1990	Miss M.Navratilova *Miss Z.L.Garrison*	2015	Miss S.J.Williams *Miss G.Muguruza*
*1903	Miss D.K.Douglass *Miss E.W.Thomson*	1933	Mrs.F.S.Moody *Miss D.E.Round*	1965	Miss M.Smith *Miss M.E.A.Bueno*	1991	Miss S.M.Graf *Miss G.B.Sabatini*	2016	Miss S.J.Williams *Miss A.Kerber*
1904	Miss D.K.Douglass *Mrs.A.Sterry*	*1934	Miss D.E.Round *Miss H.H.Jacobs*	1966	Mrs.L.W.King *Miss M.E.A.Bueno*	1992	Miss S.M.Graf *Miss M.Seles*		
1905	Miss M.G.Sutton *Miss D.K.Douglass*	1935	Mrs.F.S.Moody *Miss H.H.Jacobs*	1967	Mrs.L.W.King *Mrs.P.F.Jones*	1993	Miss S.M.Graf *Miss J.Novotna*		
1906	Miss D.K.Douglass *Miss M.G.Sutton*	*1936	Miss H.H.Jacobs *Miss S.Sperling*	1968	Mrs.L.W.King *Miss J.A.M.Tegart*	1994	Miss I.C.Martinez *Miss M.Navratilova*		
1907	Miss M.G.Sutton *Mrs.R.L.Chambers*	1937	Mrs.D.E.Round *Miss J.Jedrzejowska*	1969	Mrs.P.F.Jones *Mrs.L.W.King*	1995	Miss S.M.Graf *Miss A.I.M.Sanchez Vicario*		
*1908	Mrs.A.Sterry *Miss A.M.Morton*	*1938	Mrs.F.S.Moody *Miss H.H.Jacobs*	*1970	Mrs.B.M.Court *Mrs.L.W.King*	1996	Miss S.M.Graf *Miss A.I.M.Sanchez Vicario*		
*1909	Miss P.D.H.Boothby *Miss A.M.Morton*	*1939	Miss A.Marble *Miss K.E.Stammers*	1971	Miss E.F.Goolagong *Mrs.B.M.Court*				

MAIDEN NAMES OF LADIES' CHAMPIONS (In the tables the following have been recorded in both married and single identities)

Mrs. R. Cawley	Miss E. F. Goolagong	Mrs. G. W. Hillyard	Miss B. Bingley	Mrs. G. E. Reid	Miss K. Melville
Mrs. R. L. Chambers	Miss D. K. Douglass	Mrs. P. F. Jones	Miss A. S. Haydon	Mrs. P. D. Smylie	Miss E. M. Sayers
Mrs. B. M. Court	Miss M. Smith	Mrs. L. W. King	Miss B. J. Moffitt	Mrs. S. Sperling	Fräulein H. Krahwinkel
Mrs. B. C. Covell	Miss P. L. Howkins	Mrs. M. R. King	Miss P. E. Mudford	Mrs. A. Sterry	Miss C. R. Cooper
Mrs. D. E. Dalton	Miss J. A. M. Tegart	Mrs. D. R. Larcombe	Miss E. W. Thomson	Mrs. J. R. Susman	Miss K. Hantze
Mrs. W. du Pont	Miss M. E. Osborne	Mrs. J. M. Lloyd	Miss C. M. Evert		
Mrs. L. A. Godfree	Miss K. McKane	Mrs. F. S. Moody	Miss H. N. Wills		
Mrs. R. L. Cawley	Miss H. F. Gourlay	Mrs. O. V. Morozova	Miss O. V. Morozova		
Mrs. P-Y. Hardenne	Miss J. Henin	Mrs. L. E. G. Price	Miss S. Reynolds		

GENTLEMEN'S DOUBLES CHAMPIONS & RUNNERS-UP

1879 L.R.Erskine and H.F.Lawford *F.Durant and G.E.Tabor*	1913 H.R.Barrett and C.P.Dixon *F.W.Rahe and H.Kleinschroth*	1957 G.P.Mulloy and J.E.Patty *N.A.Fraser and L.A.Hoad*	1991 J.B.Fitzgerald and A.P.Jarryd *J.A.Frana and L.Lavalle*
1880 W.C.Renshaw and J.E.Renshaw *O.E.Woodhouse and C.J.Cole*	1914 N.E.Brookes and A.F.Wilding *H.R.Barrett and C.P.Dixon*	1958 S.V.Davidson and U.C.J.Schmidt *A.J.Cooper and N.A.Fraser*	1992 J.P.McEnroe and M.D.Stich *J.F.Grabb and R.A.Reneberg*
1881 W.C.Renshaw and J.E.Renshaw *W.J.Down and H.Vaughan*	1919 R.V.Thomas and P.O.Wood *R.Lycett and R.W.Heath*	1959 R.S.Emerson and N.A.Fraser *R.G.Laver and R.Mark*	1993 T.A.Woodbridge and M.R.Woodforde *G.D.Connell and P.J.Galbraith*
1882 J.T.Hartley and R.T.Richardson *J.G.Horn and C.B.Russell*	1920 R.N.Williams and C.S.Garland *A.R.F.Kingscote and J.C.Parke*	1960 R.H.Osuna and R.D.Ralston *M.G.Davies and R.K.Wilson*	1994 T.A.Woodbridge and M.R.Woodforde *G.D.Connell and P.J.Galbraith*
1883 C.W.Grinstead and C.E.Welldon *C.B.Russell and R.T.Milford*	1921 R.Lycett and M.Woosnam *F.G.Lowe and A.H.Lowe*	1961 R.S.Emerson and N.A.Fraser *R.A.J.Hewitt and F.S.Stolle*	1995 T.A.Woodbridge and M.R.Woodforde *R.D.Leach and S.D.Melville*
1884 W.C.Renshaw and J.E.Renshaw *E.W.Lewis and E.L.Williams*	1922 R.Lycett and J.O.Anderson *G.L.Patterson and P.O.Wood*	1962 R.A.J.Hewitt and F.S.Stolle *B.Jovanovic and N.Pilic*	1996 T.A.Woodbridge and M.R.Woodforde *B.H.Black and G.D.Connell*
1885 W.C.Renshaw and J.E.Renshaw *C.E.Farrer and A.J.Stanley*	1923 R.Lycett and L.A.Godfree *Count M.de Gomar and* *E.Flaquer*	1963 R.H.Osuna and A.Palafox *J.C.Barclay and P.Darmon*	1997 T.A.Woodbridge and M.R.Woodforde *J.F.Eltingh and P.V.N.Haarhuis*
1886 W.C.Renshaw and J.E.Renshaw *C.E.Farrer and A.J.Stanley*	1924 F.T.Hunter and V.Richards *R.N.Williams and* *W.M.Washburn*	1964 R.A.J.Hewitt and F.S.Stolle *R.S.Emerson and K.N.Fletcher*	1998 J.F.Eltingh and P.V.N.Haarhuis *T.A.Woodbridge and* *M.R.Woodforde*
1887 P.B.Lyon and H.W.W.Wilberforce *J.H.Crispe and E.Barratt-Smith*	1925 J.R.Borotra and R.Lacoste *J.F.Hennessey and R.J.Casey*	1965 J.D.Newcombe and A.D.Roche *K.N.Fletcher and R.A.J.Hewitt*	1999 M.S.Bhupathi and L.A.Paes *P.V.N.Haarhuis and J.E.Palmer*
1888 W.C.Renshaw and J.E.Renshaw *P.B.Lyon and* *H.W.W.Wilberforce*	1926 H.J.Cochet and J.Brugnon *V.Richards and H.O.Kinsey*	1966 K.N.Fletcher and J.D.Newcombe *W.W.Bowrey and O.K.Davidson*	2000 T.A.Woodbridge and M.R.Woodforde *P.V.N.Haarhuis and S.F.Stolle*
1889 W.C.Renshaw and J.E.Renshaw *E.W.Lewis and G.W.Hillyard*	1927 F.T.Hunter and W.T.Tilden *J.Brugnon and H.J.Cochet*	1967 R.A.J.Hewitt and F.D.McMillan *R.S.Emerson and K.N.Fletcher*	2001 D.J.Johnson and J.E.Palmer *J.Novak and D.Rikl*
1890 J.Pim and F.O.Stoker *E.W.Lewis and G.W.Hillyard*	1928 H.J.Cochet and J.Brugnon *G.L.Patterson and J.B.Hawkes*	1968 J.D.Newcombe and A.D.Roche *K.R.Rosewall and F.S.Stolle*	2002 J.L.Bjorkman and T.A. Woodbridge *M.S.Knowles and D.M.Nestor*
1891 W.Baddeley and H.Baddeley *J.Pim and F.O.Stoker*	1929 W.L.Allison and J.W.Van Ryn *J.C.Gregory and I.G.Collins*	1969 J.D.Newcombe and A.D.Roche *T.S.Okker and M.C.Reissen*	2003 J.L.Bjorkman and T.A. Woodbridge *M.S.Bhupathi and M.N.Mirnyi*
1892 H.S.Barlow and E.W.Lewis *W.Baddeley and H.Baddeley*	1930 W.L.Allison and J.W.Van Ryn *J.T.G.H.Doeg and G.M.Lott*	1970 J.D.Newcombe and A.D.Roche *K.R.Rosewall and F.S.Stolle*	2004 J.L.Bjorkman and T.A. Woodbridge *J.Knowle and N.Zimonjic*
1893 J.Pim and F.O.Stoker *E.W.Lewis and H.S.Barlow*	1931 G.M Lott and J.W.Van Ryn *H.J.Cochet and J.Brugnon*	1971 R.S.Emerson and R.G.Laver *A.R.Ashe and R.D.Ralston*	2005 S.W.I.Huss and W.A.Moodie *R.C.Bryan and M.C.Bryan*
1894 W.Baddeley and H.Baddeley *H.S.Barlow and C.H.Martin*	1932 J.R.Borotra and J.Brugnon *G.P.Hughes and F.J.Perry*	1972 R.A.J.Hewitt and F.D.McMillan *S.R.Smith and E.J.van Dillen*	2006 R.C.Bryan and M.C.Bryan *F.V.Santoro and N.Zimonjic*
1895 W.Baddeley and H.Baddeley *E.W.Lewis and W.V.Eaves*	1933 J.R.Borotra and J.Brugnon *R.Nunoi and J.Satoh*	1973 J.S.Connors and I.Nastase *J.R.Cooper and N.A.Fraser*	2007 A.Clement and M.Llodra *R.C.Bryan and M.C.Bryan*
1896 W.Baddeley and H.Baddeley *R.F.Doherty and H.A.Nisbet*	1934 G.M.Lott and L.R.Stoefen *J.R.Borotra and J.Brugnon*	1974 J.D.Newcombe and A.D.Roche *R.C.Lutz and S.R.Smith*	2008 D.M.Nestor and N.Zimonjic *J.L.Bjorkman and K.R.Ullyett*
1897 R.F.Doherty and H.L.Doherty *W.Baddeley and H.Baddeley*	1935 J.H.Crawford and A.K.Quist *W.L.Allison and J.W.Van Ryn*	1975 V.K.Gerulaitis and A.Mayer *C.Dowdeswell and A.J.Stone*	2009 D.M.Nestor and N.Zimonjic *R.C.Bryan and M.C.Bryan*
1898 R.F.Doherty and H.L.Doherty *H.A.Nisbet and C.Hobart*	1936 G.P.Hughes and C.R.D.Tuckey *C.E.Hare and F.H.D.Wilde*	1976 B.E.Gottfried and R.C.Ramirez *R.L.Case and G.Masters*	2010 J.Melzer and P.Petzschner *R.S.Lindstedt and H.V.Tecau*
1899 R.F.Doherty and H.L.Doherty *H.A.Nisbet and C.Hobart*	1937 J.D.Budge and G.C.Mako *G.P.Hughes and C.R.D.Tuckey*	1977 R.L.Case and G.Masters *J.G.Alexander and P.C.Dent*	2011 R.C.Bryan and M.C.Bryan *R.S.Lindstedt and H.V.Tecau*
1900 R.F.Doherty and H.L.Doherty *H.R.Barrett and H.A.Nisbet*	1938 J.D.Budge and G.C.Mako *H.E.O.Henkel and G.von Metaxa*	1978 R.A.J.Hewitt and F.D.McMillan *P.B.Fleming and J.P.McEnroe*	2012 J.F.Marray and F.L.Nielsen *R.S.Lindstedt and H.V.Tecau*
1901 R.F.Doherty and H.L.Doherty *D.Davis and H.Ward*	1939 R.L.Riggs and E.T.Cooke *C.E.Hare and F.H.D.Wilde*	1979 P.B.Fleming and J.P.McEnroe *B.E.Gottfried and R.C.Ramirez*	2013 R.C.Bryan and M.C.Bryan *I.Dodig and M.P.D.Melo*
1902 S.H.Smith and F.L.Riseley *R.F.Doherty and H.L.Doherty*	1946 T.P.Brown and J.A.Kramer *G.E.Brown and D.R.Pails*	1980 P.McNamara and P.F.McNamee *R.C.Lutz and S.R.Smith*	2014 V.Pospisil and J.E.Sock *R.C.Bryan and M.C.Bryan*
1903 R.F.Doherty and H.L.Doherty *S.H.Smith and F.L.Riseley*	1947 R.Falkenburg and J.A.Kramer *A.J.Mottram and O.W.T.Sidwell*	1981 P.B.Fleming and J.P.McEnroe *R.C.Lutz and S.R.Smith*	2015 J.J.Rojer and H.Tecau *J.R.Murray and J.Peers*
1904 R.F.Doherty and H.L.Doherty *S.H.Smith and F.L.Riseley*	1948 J.E.Bromwich and F.A.Sedgman *T.P.Brown and G.P.Mulloy*	1982 P.McNamara and P.F.McNamee *P.B.Fleming and J.P.McEnroe*	2016 P-H.Herbert and N.P.A.Mahut *J.Benneteau and E.Roger-* *Vasselin*
1905 R.F.Doherty and H.L.Doherty *S.H.Smith and F.L.Riseley*	1949 R.A.Gonzales and F.A.Parker *G.P.Mulloy and F.R.Schroeder*	1983 P.B.Fleming and J.P.McEnroe *T.E.Gullikson and T.R.Gullikson*	
1906 S.H.Smith and F.L.Riseley *R.F.Doherty and H.L.Doherty*	1950 J.E.Bromwich and A.K.Quist *G.E.Brown and O.W.T.Sidwell*	1984 P.B.Fleming and J.P.McEnroe *P.Cash and P.McNamee*	
1907 N.E.Brookes and A.F.Wilding *B.C.Wright and K.Behr*	1951 K.B.McGregor and F.A.Sedgman *J.Drobny and E.W.Sturgess*	1985 H.P.Guenthardt and B.Taroczy *P.H.Cash and J.B.Fitzgerald*	
1908 A.F.Wilding and M.J.G.Ritchie *A.W.Gore and H.R.Barrett*	1952 K.B.McGregor and F.A.Sedgman *E.V.Seixas and E.W.Sturgess*	1986 T.K.Nystrom and M.A.O.Wilander *G.W.Donnelly and P.B.Fleming*	
1909 A.W.Gore and H.R.Barrett *S.N.Doust and H.A.Parker*	1953 L.A.Hoad and K.R.Rosewall *R.N.Hartwig and M.G.Rose*	1987 K.E.Flach and R.A.Seguso *S.Casal and E.Sanchez*	
1910 A.F.Wilding and M.J.G.Ritchie *A.W.Gore and H.R.Barrett*	1954 R.N.Hartwig and M.G.Rose *E.V.Seixas and M.A.Trabert*	1988 K.E.Flach and R.A.Seguso *J.B.Fitzgerald and A.P.Jarryd*	
1911 M.O.M.Decugis and A.H.Gobert *M.J.G.Ritchie and A.F.Wilding*	1955 R.N.Hartwig and L.A.Hoad *N.A.Fraser and K.R.Rosewall*	1989 J.B.Fitzgerald and A.P.Jarryd *R.D.Leach and J.R.Pugh*	
1912 H.R.Barrett and C.P.Dixon *M.O.Decugis and A.H.Gobert*	1956 L.A.Hoad and K.R.Rosewall *N.Pietrangeli and O.Sirola*	1990 R.D.Leach and J.R.Pugh *P.Aldrich and D.T.Visser*	

LADIES' DOUBLES CHAMPIONS & RUNNERS-UP

1913	Mrs.R.J.McNair and Miss P.D.H.Boothby *Mrs.A.Sterry and Mrs.R.L.Chambers*
1914	Miss E.M.Ryan and Miss A.M.Morton *Mrs.D.T.R.Larcombe and Mrs.F.J.Hannam*
1919	Miss S.R.F.Lenglen and Miss E.M.Ryan *Mrs.R.L.Chambers and Mrs.D.T.R.Larcombe*
1920	Miss S.R.F.Lenglen and Miss E.M.Ryan *Mrs.R.L.Chambers and Mrs.D.T.R.Larcombe*
1921	Miss S.R.F.Lenglen and Miss E.M.Ryan *Mrs.A.E.Beamish and Mrs.G.E.Peacock*
1922	Miss S.R.F.Lenglen and Miss E.M.Ryan *Mrs.A.D.Stocks and Miss K.McKane*
1923	Miss S.R.F.Lenglen and Miss E.M.Ryan *Miss J.W.Austin and Miss E.L.Colyer*
1924	Mrs.G.Wightman and Miss H.Wills *Mrs.B.C.Covell and Miss K.McKane*
1925	Miss S.Lenglen and Miss E.Ryan *Mrs.A.V.Bridge and Mrs.C.G.McIlquham*
1926	Miss E.M.Ryan and Miss M.K.Browne *Mrs.L.A.Godfree and Miss E.L.Colyer*
1927	Miss H.N.Wills and Miss E.M.Ryan *Miss E.L.Heine and Mrs.G.E.Peacock*
1928	Mrs.M.R.Watson and Miss M.A.Saunders *Miss E.H.Harvey and Miss E.Bennett*
1929	Mrs.M.R.Watson and Mrs.L.R.C.Michell *Mrs.B.C.Covell and Mrs.W.P.Barron*
1930	Mrs.F.S.Moody and Miss E.M.Ryan *Miss E.A.Cross and Miss S.H.Palfrey*
1931	Mrs.D.C.Shepherd-Barron and Miss P.E.Mudford *Miss D.E.Metaxa and Miss J.Sigart*
1932	Miss D.E.Metaxa and Miss J.Sigart *Miss E.M.Ryan and Miss H.H.Jacobs*
1933	Mrs.R.Mathieu and Miss E.M.Ryan *Miss W.A.James and Miss A.M.Yorke*
1934	Mrs.R.Mathieu and Miss E.M.Ryan *Mrs.D.B.Andrus and Mrs.C.F.Henrotin*
1935	Miss W.A.James and Miss K.E.Stammers *Mrs.R.Mathieu and Mrs.S.Sperling*
1936	Miss W.A.James and Miss K.E.Stammers *Mrs.M.Fabyan and Miss H.H.Jacobs*
1937	Mrs.R.Mathieu and Miss A.M.Yorke *Mrs.M.R.King and Mrs.J.B.Pittman*
1938	Mrs.M.Fabyan and Miss A.Marble *Mrs.R.Mathieu and Miss A.M.Yorke*
1939	Mrs.M.Fabyan and Miss A.Marble *Miss H.H.Jacobs and Miss A.M.Yorke*
1946	Miss A.L.Brough and Miss M.E.Osborne *Miss P.M.Betz and Miss D.J.Hart*
1947	Miss D.J.Hart and Mrs.R.B.Todd *Miss A.L.Brough and Miss M.E.Osborne*
1948	Miss A.L.Brough and Mrs.W.du Pont *Miss D.J.Hart and Mrs.R.B.Todd*
1949	Miss A.L.Brough and Mrs.W.du Pont *Miss G.Moran and Mrs.R.B.Todd*
1950	Miss A.L.Brough and Mrs.W.du Pont *Miss S.J.Fry and Miss D.J.Hart*
1951	Miss S.J.Fry and Miss D.J.Hart *Miss A.L.Brough and Mrs.W.du Pont*
1952	Miss S.J.Fry and Miss D.J.Hart *Miss A.L.Brough and Miss M.C.Connolly*
1953	Miss S.J.Fry and Miss D.J.Hart *Miss M.C.Connolly and Miss J.A.Sampson*
1954	Miss A.L.Brough and Mrs.W.du Pont *Miss S.J.Fry and Miss D.J.Hart*
1955	Miss F.A.Mortimer and Miss J.A.Shilcock *Miss S.J.Bloomer and Miss P.E.Ward*
1956	Miss A.Buxton and Miss A.Gibson *Miss E.F.Muller and Miss D.G.Seeney*
1957	Miss A.Gibson and Miss D.R.Hard *Mrs.K.Hawton and Mrs.M.N.Long*
1958	Miss M.E.A.Bueno and Miss A.Gibson *Mrs.W.du Pont and Miss M.Varner*
1959	Miss J.M.Arth and Miss D.R.Hard *Mrs.J.G.Fleitz and Miss C.C.Truman*
1960	Miss M.E.A.Bueno and Miss D.R.Hard *Miss S.Reynolds and Miss R.Schuurman*
1961	Miss K.J.Hantze and Miss B.J.Moffitt *Miss J.P.Lehane and Miss M.Smith*
1962	Miss B.J.Moffitt and Mrs.J.R.Susman *Mrs.L.E.G.Price and Miss R.Schuurman*
1963	Miss M.E.A.Bueno and Miss D.R.Hard *Miss R.A.Ebbern and Miss M.Smith*
1964	Miss M.Smith and Miss L.R.Turner *Miss B.J.Moffitt and Mrs.J.R.Susman*
1965	Miss M.E.A.Bueno and Miss B.J.Moffitt *Miss F.G.Durr and Miss J.P.Lieffrig*
1966	Miss M.E.A.Bueno and Miss N.A.Richey *Miss M.Smith and Miss J.A.M.Tegart*
1967	Miss R.Casals and Mrs.L.W.King *Miss M.E.A.Bueno and Miss N.A.Richey*
1968	Miss R.Casals and Mrs.L.W.King *Miss F.G.Durr and Mrs.P.F.Jones*
1969	Mrs.B.M.Court and Miss J.A.M.Tegart *Miss P.S.A.Hogan and Miss M.Michel*
1970	Miss R.Casals and Mrs.L.W.King *Miss F.G.Durr and Miss S.V.Wade*
1971	Miss R.Casals and Mrs.L.W.King *Mrs.B.M.Court and Miss E.F.Goolagong*
1972	Mrs.L.W.King and Miss B.F.Stove *Mrs.D.E.Dalton and Miss F.G.Durr*
1973	Miss R.Casals and Mrs.L.W.King *Miss F.G.Durr and Miss B.F.Stove*
1974	Miss E.F.Goolagong and Miss M.Michel *Miss H.F.Gourlay and Miss K.M.Krantzcke*
1975	Miss A.K.Kiyomura and Miss K.Sawamatsu *Miss F.G.Durr and Miss B.F.Stove*
1976	Miss C.M.Evert and Miss M.Navratilova *Mrs.L.W.King and Miss B.F.Stove*
1977	Mrs.R.L.Cawley and Miss J.C.Russell *Miss M.Navratilova and Miss B.F.Stove*
1978	Mrs.G.E.Reid and Miss W.M.Turnbull *Miss M.Jausovec and Miss V.Ruzici*
1979	Mrs.L.W.King and Miss M.Navratilova *Miss B.F.Stove and Miss W.M.Turnbull*
1980	Miss K.Jordan and Miss A.E.Smith *Miss R.Casals and Miss W.M.Turnbull*
1981	Miss M.Navratilova and Miss P.H.Shriver *Miss K.Jordan and Miss A.E.Smith*
1982	Miss M.Navratilova and Miss P.H.Shriver *Miss K.Jordan and Miss A.E.Smith*
1983	Miss M.Navratilova and Miss P.H.Shriver *Miss R.Casals and Miss W.M.Turnbull*
1984	Miss M.Navratilova and Miss P.H.Shriver *Miss K.Jordan and Miss A.E.Smith*
1985	Miss K.Jordan and Mrs.P.D.Smylie *Miss M.Navratilova and Miss P.H.Shriver*
1986	Miss M.Navratilova and Miss P.H.Shriver *Miss H.Mandlikova and Miss W.M.Turnbull*
1987	Miss C.G.Kohde-Kilsch and Miss H.Sukova *Miss H.E.Nagelsen and Mrs.P.D.Smylie*
1988	Miss S.M.Graf and Miss G.B.Sabatini *Miss L.I.Savchenko and Miss N.M.Zvereva*
1989	Miss J.Novotna and Miss H.Sukova *Miss L.I.Savchenko and Miss N.M.Zvereva*
1990	Miss J.Novotna and Miss H.Sukova *Miss K.Jordan and Mrs.P.D.Smylie*
1991	Miss L.I.Savchenko and Miss N.M.Zvereva *Miss B.C.Fernandez and Miss J.Novotna*
1992	Miss B.C.Fernandez and Miss N.M.Zvereva *Miss J.Novotna and Mrs.A.Neiland*
1993	Miss B.C.Fernandez and Miss N.M.Zvereva *Mrs.A.Neiland and Miss J.Novotna*
1994	Miss B.C.Fernandez and Miss N.M.Zvereva *Miss J.Novotna and Miss A.I.M.Sanchez Vicario*
1995	Miss J.Novotna and Miss A.I.M.Sanchez Vicario *Miss B.C.Fernandez and Miss N.M.Zvereva*
1996	Miss M.Hingis and Miss H.Sukova *Miss M.J.McGrath and Mrs.A.Neiland*
1997	Miss B.C.Fernandez and Miss N.M.Zvereva *Miss N.J.Arendt and Miss M.M.Bollegraf*
1998	Miss M.Hingis and Miss J.Novotna *Miss L.A.Davenport and Miss N.M.Zvereva*
1999	Miss L.A.Davenport and Miss C.M.Morariu *Miss M.de Swardt and Miss E.Tatarkova*
2000	Miss S.J.Williams and Miss V.E.S.Williams *Mrs.A.Decugis and Miss A.Sugiyama*
2001	Miss L.M.Raymond and Miss R.P.Stubbs *Miss K.Clijsters and Miss A.Sugiyama*
2002	Miss S.J.Williams and Miss V.E.S.Williams *Miss V.Ruano Pascual and Miss P.L.Suarez*
2003	Miss K.Clijsters and Miss A.Sugiyama *Miss V.Ruano Pascual and Miss P.L.Suarez*
2004	Miss C.C.Black and Miss R.P.Stubbs *Mrs.A.Huber and Miss A.Sugiyama*
2005	Miss C.C.Black and Mrs.A.Huber *Miss S.Kuznetsova and Miss A.Muresmo*
2006	Miss Z.Yan and Miss J.Zheng *Miss V.Ruano Pascual and Miss P.L.Suarez*
2007	Miss C.C.Black and Mrs.A.Huber *Miss K.Srebotnik and Miss A.Sugiyama*
2008	Miss S.J.Williams and Miss V.E.S.Williams *Miss L.M.Raymond and Miss S.J.Stosur*
2009	Miss S.J.Williams and Miss V.E.S.Williams *Miss S.J.Stosur and Miss R.P.Stubbs*
2010	Miss V.King and Miss Y.V.Shvedova *Miss E.S.Vesnina and Miss V.Zvonareva*
2011	Miss K.Peschke and Miss K.Srebotnik *Miss S.Lisicki and Miss S.J.Stosur*
2012	Miss S.J.Williams and Miss V.E.S.Williams *Miss A.Hlavackova and Miss L.Hradecka*
2013	Miss S-W.Hsieh and Miss S.Peng *Miss A.Barty and Miss C.Dellacqua*
2014	Miss S.Errani and Miss R.Vinci *Miss T.Babos and Miss K.Mladenovic*
2015	Miss M.Hingis and Miss S.Mirza *Miss E.Makarova and Miss E.S.Vesnina*
2016	Miss S.J.Williams and Miss V.E.S.Williams *Miss T.Babos and Miss Y.Shvedova*

MIXED DOUBLES CHAMPIONS & RUNNERS-UP

1913   H.Crisp and Mrs.C.O.Tuckey
J.C.Parke and Mrs.D.T.R.Larcombe

1914   J.C.Parke and Mrs.D.T.R.Larcombe
A.F.Wilding and Miss M.Broquedis

1919   R.Lycett and Miss E.M.Ryan
A.D.Prebble and Mrs.R.L.Chambers

1920   G.L.Patterson and Miss S.R.F.Lenglen
R.Lycett and Miss E.M.Ryan

1921   R.Lycett and Miss E.M.Ryan
M.Woosnam and Miss P.L.Howkins

1922   P.O.Wood and Miss S.R.F.Lenglen
R.Lycett and Miss E.M.Ryan

1923   R.Lycett and Miss E.M.Ryan
L.S.Deane and Mrs.W.P.Barron

1924   J.B.Gilbert and Miss K.McKane
L.A.Godfree and Mrs.W.P.Barron

1925   J.Borotra and Miss S.R.F.Lenglen
U.L.de Morpurgo and Miss E.M.Ryan

1926   L.A.Godfree and Mrs.L.A.Godfree
H.O.Kinsey and Miss M.K.Browne

1927   F.T.Hunter and Miss E.M.Ryan
L.A.Godfree and Mrs.L.A.Godfree

1928   P.D.B.Spence and Miss E.M.Ryan
J.H.Crawford and Miss D.J.Akhurst

1929   F.T.Hunter and Miss H.N.Wills
I.G.Collins and Miss J.C.Fry

1930   J.H.Crawford and Miss E.M.Ryan
D.D.Prenn and Miss H.Krahwinkel

1931   G.M.Lott and Mrs.L.A.Harper
I.G.Collins and Miss J.C.Ridley

1932   E.G.Maier and Miss E.M.Ryan
H.C.Hopman and Miss J.Sigart

1933   G.von Cramm and Miss H.Krahwinkel
N.G.Farquharson and Miss G.M.Heeley

1934   R.Miki and Miss D.E.Round
H.W.Austin and Mrs.W.P.Barron

1935   F.J.Perry and Miss D.E.Round
H.C.Hopman and Mrs.H.C.Hopman

1936   F.J.Perry and Miss D.E.Round
J.D.Budge and Mrs.M.Fabyan

1937   J.D.Budge and Miss A.Marble
Y.F.M.Petra and Mrs.R.Mathieu

1938   J.D.Budge and Miss A.Marble
H.E.O.Henkel and Mrs.M.Fabyan

1939   R.L.Riggs and Miss A.Marble
F.H.D.Wilde and Miss N.B.Brown

1946   T.P.Brown and Miss A.L.Brough
G.E.Brown and Miss D.M.Bundy

1947   J.E.Bromwich and Miss A.L.Brough
C.F.Long and Mrs.G.F.Bolton

1948   J.E.Bromwich and Miss A.L.Brough
F.A.Sedgman and Miss D.J.Hart

1949   E.W.Sturgess and Mrs.R.A.Summers
J.E.Bromwich and Miss A.L.Brough

1950   E.W.Sturgess and Miss A.L.Brough
G.E.Brown and Mrs.R.B.Todd

1951   F.A.Sedgman and Miss D.J.Hart
M.G.Rose and Mrs.G.F.Bolton

1952   F.A.Sedgman and Miss D.J.Hart
E.J.Morea and Mrs.M.N.Long

1953   E.V.Seixas and Miss D.J.Hart
E.J.Morea and Miss S.J.Fry

1954   E.V.Seixas and Miss D.J.Hart
K.R.Rosewall and Mrs.W.du Pont

1955   E.V.Seixas and Miss D.J.Hart
E.J.Morea and Miss A.L.Brough

1956   E.V.Seixas and Miss S.J.Fry
G.P.Mulloy and Miss A.Gibson

1957   M.G.Rose and Miss D.R.Hard
N.A.Fraser and Miss A.Gibson

1958   R.N.Howe and Miss L.Coghlan
K.Nielsen and Miss A.Gibson

1959   R.G.Laver and Miss D.R.Hard
N.A.Fraser and Miss M.E.A.Bueno

1960   R.G.Laver and Miss D.R.Hard
R.N.Howe and Miss M.E.A.Bueno

1961   F.S.Stolle and Miss L.R.Turner
R.N.Howe and Miss E.Buding

1962   N.A.Fraser and Mrs.W.du Pont
R.D.Ralston and Miss A.S.Haydon

1963   K.N.Fletcher and Miss M.Smith
R.A.J.Hewitt and Miss D.R.Hard

1964   F.S.Stolle and Miss L.R.Turner
K.N.Fletcher and Miss M.Smith

1965   K.N.Fletcher and Miss M.Smith
A.D.Roche and Miss J.A.M.Tegart

1966   K.N.Fletcher and Miss M.Smith
R.D.Ralston and Mrs.L.W.King

1967   O.K.Davidson and Mrs.L.W.King
K.N.Fletcher and Miss M.E.A.Bueno

1968   K.N.Fletcher and Mrs.B.M.Court
A.Metreveli and Miss O.V.Morozova

1969   F.S.Stolle and Mrs.P.F.Jones
A.D.Roche and Miss J.A.M.Tegart

1970   I.Nastase and Miss R.Casals
A.Metreveli and Miss O.V.Morozova

1971   O.K.Davidson and Mrs.L.W.King
M.C.Riessen and Mrs.B.M.Court

1972   I.Nastase and Miss R.Casals
K.G.Warwick and Miss E.F.Goolagong

1973   O.K.Davidson and Mrs.L.W.King
R.C.Ramirez and Miss J.S.Newberry

1974   O.K.Davidson and Mrs.L.W.King
M.J.Farrell and Miss L.J.Charles

1975   M.C.Riessen and Mrs.B.M.Court
A.J.Stone and Miss B.F.Stove

1976   A.D.Roche and Miss F.G.Durr
R.L.Stockton and Miss R.Casals

1977   R.A.J.Hewitt and Miss G.R.Stevens
F.D.McMillan and Miss B.F.Stove

1978   F.D.McMillan and Miss B.F.Stove
R.O.Ruffels and Mrs.L.W.King

1979   R.A.J.Hewitt and Miss G.R.Stevens
F.D.McMillan and Miss B.F.Stove

1980   J.R.Austin and Miss T.A.Austin
M.R.Edmondson and Miss D.L.Fromholtz

1981   F.D.McMillan and Miss B.F.Stove
J.R.Austin and Miss T.A.Austin

1982   K.M.Curren and Miss A.E.Smith
J.M.Lloyd and Miss W.M.Turnbull

1983   J.M.Lloyd and Miss W.M.Turnbull
S.B.Denton and Mrs.L.W.King

1984   J.M.Lloyd and Miss W.M.Turnbull
S.B.Denton and Miss K.Jordan

1985   P.F.McNamee and Miss M.Navratilova
J.B.Fitzgerald and Mrs.P.D.Smylie

1986   K.E.Flach and Miss K.Jordan
H.P.Guenthardt and Miss M.Navratilova

1987   M.J.Bates and Miss J.M.Durie
D.A.Cahill and Miss N.A-L.Provis

1988   S.E.Stewart and Miss Z.L.Garrison
K.L.Jones and Mrs.S.W.Magers

1989   J.R.Pugh and Miss J.Novotna
M.Kratzmann and Miss J.M.Byrne

1990   R.D.Leach and Miss Z.L.Garrison
J.B.Fitzgerald and Mrs.P.D.Smylie

1991   J.B.Fitzgerald and Mrs.P.D.Smylie
J.R.Pugh and Miss N.M.Zvereva

1992   C.Suk and Mrs.A.Neiland
J.F.Eltingh and Miss M.J.M.M.Oremans

1993   M.R.Woodforde and Miss M.Navratilova
T.J.C.M.Nijssen and Miss M.M.Bollegraf

1994   T.A.Woodbridge and Miss H.Sukova
T.J.Middleton and Miss L.M.McNeil

1995   J.A.Stark and Miss M.Navratilova
C.Suk and Miss B.C.Fernandez

1996   C.Suk and Miss H.Sukova
M.R.Woodforde and Mrs.A.Neiland

1997   C.Suk and Miss H.Sukova
A.Olhovskiy and Mrs.A.Neiland

1998   M.N.Mirnyi and Miss S.J.Williams
M.S.Bhupathi and Miss M.Lucic

1999   L.A.Paes and Miss L.M.Raymond
J.L.Bjorkman and Miss A.S.Kournikova

2000   D.J.Johnson and Miss K.Y.Po
L.G.Hewitt and Miss K.Clijsters

2001   L.Friedl and Miss D.Hantuchova
M.C.Bryan and Mrs.A.Huber

2002   M.S.Bhupathi and Miss E.A.Likhovtseva
K.R.Ullyett and Miss D.Hantuchova

2003   L.A.Paes and Miss M.Navratilova
A.Ram and Miss A.Rodionova

2004   W.Black and Miss C.C.Black
T.A.Woodbridge and Miss A.H.Molik

2005   M.S.Bhupathi and Miss M.C.Pierce
P.Hanley and Miss T.Perebiynis

2006   A.Ram and Miss V.Zvonareva
R.C.Bryan and Miss V.E.S.Williams

2007   J.R.Murray and Miss J.Jankovic
J.L.Bjorkman and Miss A.H.Molik

2008   R.C.Bryan and Miss S.J.Stosur
M.C.Bryan and Miss K.Srebotnik

2009   M.S.Knowles and Miss A-L.Groenefeld
L.A.Paes and Miss C.C.Black

2010   L.A.Paes and Miss C.C.Black
W.A.Moodie and Miss L.M.Raymond

2011   J.Melzer and Miss I.Benesova
M.S.Bhupathi and Miss E.S.Vesnina

2012   M.Bryan and Miss L.M.Raymond
L.A.Paes and Miss E.S.Vesnina

2013   D.M.Nestor and Miss K.Mladenovic
B.Soares and Miss L.M.Raymond

2014   N.Zimonjic and Miss S.Stosur
M.N.Mirnyi and Miss H.Chan

2015   L.A.Paes and Miss M.Hingis
A.Peya and Miss T.Babos

2016   H.Kontinen and Miss H.M.Watson
R.F.Farah and Miss A-L.Groenefeld

BOYS' SINGLES

1947	K.Nielsen *S.V.Davidson*	1965	V.Korotkov *G.Goven*
1948	S.O.Stockenberg *D.Vad*	1966	V.Korotkov *B.E.Fairlie*
1949	S.O.Stockenberg *J.A.T.Horn*	1967	M.Orantes *M.S.Estep*

1947 K.Nielsen
S.V.Davidson
1948 S.O.Stockenberg
D.Vad
1949 S.O.Stockenberg
J.A.T.Horn
1950 J.A.T.Horn
K.Mobarek
1951 J.Kupferburger
K.Mobarek
1952 R.K.Wilson
T.T.Fancutt
1953 W.A.Knight
R.Krishnan
1954 R.Krishnan
A.J.Cooper
1955 M.P.Hann
J.E.Lundquist
1956 R.E.Holmberg
R.G.Laver
1957 J.I.Tattersall
I.Ribeiro
1958 E.H.Buchholz
P.J.Lall
1959 T.Lejus
R.W.Barnes
1960 A.R.Mandelstam
J.Mukerjea
1961 C.E.Graebner
E.Blanke
1962 S.J.Matthews
A.Metreveli
1963 N.Kalogeropoulos
I.El Shafei
1964 I.El Shafei
V.Korotkov

1965 V.Korotkov
G.Goven
1966 V.Korotkov
B.E.Fairlie
1967 M.Orantes
M.S.Estep
1968 J.G.Alexander
J.Thamin
1969 B.M.Bertram
J.G.Alexander
1970 B.M.Bertram
F.Gebert
1971 R.I.Kreiss
S.A.Warboys
1972 B.R.Borg
C.J.Mottram
1973 W.W.Martin
C.S.Dowdeswell
1974 W.W.Martin
Ash Amritraj
1975 C.J.Lewis
R.Ycaza
1976 H.P.Guenthardt
P.Elter
1977 V.A.W.Winitsky
T.E.Teltscher
1978 I.Lendl
J.Turpin
1979 R.Krishnan
D.Siegler
1980 T.Tulasne
H.D.Beutel
1981 M.W.Anger
P.H.Cash
1982 P.H.Cash
H.Sundstrom

1983 S.B.Edberg
J.Frawley
1984 M.Kratzmann
S.Kruger
1985 L.Lavalle
E.Velez
1986 E.Velez
J.Sanchez
1987 D.Nargiso
J.R.Stoltenberg
1988 N.Pereira
G.Raoux
1989 L.J.N.Kulti
T.A.Woodbridge
1990 L.A.Paes
M.Ondruska
1991 K.J.T.Enquist
M.Joyce
1992 D.Skoch
B.Dunn
1993 R.Sabau
J.Szymanski
1994 S.M.Humphries
M.A.Philippoussis
1995 O.Mutis
N.Kiefer
1996 V.Voltchkov
I.Ljubicic
1997 W.Whitehouse
D.Elsner
1998 R.Federer
I.Labadze
1999 J.Melzer
K.Pless
2000 N.P.A.Mahut
M.Ancic

2001 R.Valent
G.Muller
2002 T.C.Reid
L.Quahab
2003 F.Mergea
C.Guccione
2004 G.Monfils
M.Kasiri
2005 J.Chardy
R.Haase
2006 T.De Bakker
M.Gawron
2007 D.Young
V.Ignatic
2008 G.Dimitrov
H.Kontinen
2009 A.Kuznetsov
J.Cox
2010 M.Fucsovics
B.Mitchell
2011 L.Saville
L.Broady
2012 F.Peliwo
L.Saville
2013 G.Quinzi
H.Chung
2014 N.Rubin
S.Kozlov
2015 R.Opelka
M.Ymer
2016 D.Shapovalov
A.De Minaur

BOYS' DOUBLES

1982 P.H.Cash and J.Frawley
R.D.Leach and J.J.Ross
1983 M.Kratzmann and S.Youl
M.Nastase and O.Rahnasto
1984 R.Brown and R.V.Weiss
M.Kratzmann and J.Svensson
1985 A.Moreno and J.Yzaga
P.Korda and C.Suk
1986 T.Carbonell and P.Korda
S.Barr and H.Karrasch
1987 J.Stoltenberg and T.A.Woodbridge
D.Nargiso and E.Rossi
1988 J.R.Stoltenberg and T.A.Woodbridge
D.Rikl and T.Zdrazila
1989 J.E.Palmer and J.A.Stark
J-L.De Jager and W.R.Ferreira
1990 S.Lareau and S.Leblanc
C.Marsh and M.Ondruska
1991 K.Alami and G.Rusedski
J-L.De Jager and A.Medvedev
1992 S.Baldas and S.Draper
M.S.Bhupathi and N.Kirtane
1993 S.Downs and J.Greenhalgh
N.Godwin and G.Williams
1994 B.Ellwood and M.Philippoussis
V.Platenik and R.Schlachter

1995 J.Lee and J.M.Trotman
A.Hernandez and M.Puerta
1996 D.Bracciali and J.Robichaud
D.Roberts and W.Whitehouse
1997 L.Horna and N.Massu
J.Van de Westhuizen
and W.Whitehouse
1998 R.Federer and O.L.P.Rochus
M.Llodra and A.Ram
1999 G.Coria and D.P.Nalbandian
T.Enev and J.Nieminem
2000 D.Coene and K.Vliegen
A.Banks and B.Riby
2001 F.Dancevic and G.Lapentti
B.Echagaray and S.Gonzales
2002 F.Mergea and H.V.Tecau
B.Baker and B.Ram
2003 F.Mergea and H.V.Tecau
A.Feeney and C.Guccione
2004 B.Evans and S.Oudsema
R.Haase and V.Troicki
2005 J.Levine and M.Shabaz
S.Groth and A.Kennaugh
2006 K.Damico and N.Schnugg
M.Klizan and A.Martin

2007 D.Lopez and M.Trevisan
R.Jebavy and M.Klizan
2008 C-P.Hsieh and T-H.Yang
M.Reid and B.Tomic
2009 P-H.Herbert and K.Krawietz
J.Obry and A.Puget
2010 L.Broady and T.Farquharson
L.Burton and G.Morgan
2011 G.Morgan and M.Pavic
O.Golding and J.Vesely
2012 A.Harris and N.Kyrgios
M.Donati and P.Licciardi
2013 T.Kokkinakis and N.Kyrgios
E.Couacaud and S.Napolitano
2014 O.Luz and M.Zormann
S.Kozlov and A.Rublev
2015 N.H.Ly and S.Nagal
R.Opelka and A.Santillan
2016 K.Raisma and S.Tsitsipas
F.Auger-Aliassime and D.Shapovalov

GIRLS' SINGLES

1947 Miss G.Domken	1965 Miss O.V.Morozova	1983 Miss P.Paradis	2001 Miss A.Widjaja
Miss B.Wallen	*Miss R.Giscarfe*	*Miss P.Hy*	*Miss D.Safina*
1948 Miss O.Miskova	1966 Miss B.Lindstrom	1984 Miss A.N.Croft	2002 Miss V.Douchevina
Miss V.Rigollet	*Miss J.A.Congdon*	*Miss E.Reinach*	*Miss M.Sharapova*
1949 Miss C.Mercelis	1967 Miss J.H.Salome	1985 Miss A.Holikova	2003 Miss K.Flipkens
Miss J.S.V.Partridge	*Miss E.M.Strandberg*	*Miss J.M.Byrne*	*Miss A.Tchakvetadze*
1950 Miss L.Cornell	1968 Miss K.S.Pigeon	1986 Miss N.M.Zvereva	2004 Miss K.Bondarenko
Miss A.Winter	*Miss L.E.Hunt*	*Miss L.Meskhi*	*Miss A.Ivanovic*
1951 Miss L.Cornell	1969 Miss K.Sawamatsu	1987 Miss N.M.Zvereva	2005 Miss A.R.Radwanska
Miss S.Lazzarino	*Miss B.I.Kirk*	*Miss J.Halard*	*Miss T.Paszek*
1952 Miss F.J.I.ten Bosch	1970 Miss S.A.Walsh	1988 Miss B.A.M.Schultz	2006 Miss C.Wozniacki
Miss R.Davar	*Miss M.V.Kroshina*	*Miss E.Derly*	*Miss M.Rybarikova*
1953 Miss D.Kilian	1971 Miss M.V.Kroschina	1989 Miss A.Strnadova	2007 Miss U.Radwanska
Miss V.A.Pitt	*Miss S.H.Minford*	*Miss M.J.McGrath*	*Miss M.Brengle*
1954 Miss V.A.Pitt	1972 Miss I.S.Kloss	1990 Miss A.Strnadova	2008 Miss L.M.D.Robson
Miss C.Monnot	*Miss G.L.Coles*	*Miss K.Sharpe*	*Miss N.Lertcheewakarn*
1955 Miss S.M.Armstrong	1973 Miss A.K.Kiyomura	1991 Miss B.Rittner	2009 Miss N.Lertcheewakarn
Miss B.de Chambure	*Miss M.Navratilova*	*Miss E.Makarova*	*Miss K.Mladenovic*
1956 Miss A.S.Haydon	1974 Miss M.Jausovec	1992 Miss C.R.Rubin	2010 Miss K.Pliskova
Miss I.Buding	*Miss M.Simionescu*	*Miss L.Courtois*	*Miss S.Ishizu*
1957 Miss M.G.Arnold	1975 Miss N.Y.Chmyreva	1993 Miss N.Feber	2011 Miss A.Barty
Miss E.Reyes	*Miss R.Marsikova*	*Miss R.Grande*	*Miss I.Khromacheva*
1958 Miss S.M.Moore	1976 Miss N.Y.Chmyreva	1994 Miss M.Hingis	2012 Miss E.Bouchard
Miss A.Dmitrieva	*Miss M.Kruger*	*Miss M-R.Jeon*	*Miss E.Svitolina*
1959 Miss J.Cross	1977 Miss L.Antonoplis	1995 Miss A.Olsza	2013 Miss B.Bencic
Miss D.Schuster	*Miss M.Louie*	*Miss T.Tanasugarn*	*Miss T.Townsend*
1960 Miss K.J.Hantze	1978 Miss T.A.Austin	1996 Miss A.Mauresmo	2014 Miss J.Ostapenko
Miss L.M.Hutchings	*Miss H.Mandlikova*	*Miss M.L.Serna*	*Miss K.Schmiedlova*
1961 Miss G.Baksheeva	1979 Miss M.L.Piatek	1997 Miss C.C.Black	2015 Miss S.Zhuk
Miss K.D.Chabot	*Miss A.A.Moulton*	*Miss A.Rippner*	*Miss A.Blinkova*
1962 Miss G.Baksheeva	1980 Miss D.Freeman	1998 Miss K.Srebotnik	2016 Miss A.S.Potapova
Miss E.P.Terry	*Miss S.J.Leo*	*Miss K.Clijsters*	*Miss D.O.Yastremska*
1963 Miss D.M.Salfati	1981 Miss Z.L.Garrison	1999 Miss I.Tulyagnova	
Miss K.Dening	*Miss R.R.Uys*	*Miss L.Krasnoroutskaya*	
1964 Miss J.M.Bartkowicz	1982 Miss C.Tanvier	2000 Miss M.E.Salerni	
Miss E.Subirats	*Miss H.Sukova*	*Miss T.Perebiynis*	

GIRLS' DOUBLES

1982 Miss E.A.Herr and Miss P.Barg	1994 Miss E.De Villiers and Miss E.E.Jelfs	2005 Miss V.A.Azarenka and Miss A.Szavay
Miss B.S.Gerken and Miss G.A.Rush	*Miss C.M.Morariu and Miss L.Varmuzova*	*Miss M.Erakovic and Miss M.Niculescu*
1983 Miss P.A.Fendick and Miss P.Hy	1995 Miss C.C.Black and Miss A.Olsza	2006 Miss A.Kleybanova and Miss A.Pavlyuchenkova
Miss C.Anderholm and Miss H.Olsson	*Miss T.Musgrove and Miss J. Richardson*	*Miss K.Antoniychuk and Miss A.Dulgheru*
1984 Miss C.Kuhlman and Miss S.C.Rehe	1996 Miss O.Barabanschikova and Miss A.Mauresmo	2007 Miss A.Pavlyuchenkova and Miss U.Radwanska
Miss V.Milvidskaya and Miss L.I.Savchenko	*Miss L.Osterloh and Miss S.Reeves*	*Miss M.Doi and Miss K.Nara*
1985 Miss L.Field and Miss J.G.Thompson	1997 Miss C.C.Black and Miss I.Selyutina	2008 Miss P.Hercog and Miss J.Moore
Miss E.Reinach and Miss J.A.Richardson	*Miss M.Matevzic and Miss K.Srebotnik*	*Miss I.Holland and Miss S.Peers*
1986 Miss M.Jaggard and Miss L.O'Neill	1998 Miss E.Dyrberg and Miss J.Kostanic	2009 Miss N.Lertcheewakarn and Miss S.Peers
Miss L.Meskhi and Miss N.M.Zvereva	*Miss P.Rampre and Miss I.Tulyaganova*	*Miss K.Mladenovic and Miss S.Njiric*
1987 Miss N.Medvedeva and Miss N.M.Zvereva	1999 Miss D.Bedanova and Miss M.E.Salerni	2010 Miss T.Babos and Miss S.Stephens
Miss I.S.Kim and Miss P.M.Moreno	*Miss T.Perebiynis and Miss I.Tulyaganova*	*Miss I.Khromacheva and Miss E.Svitolina*
1988 Miss J.A.Faull and Miss R.McQuillan	2000 Miss I.Gaspar and Miss T.Perebiynis	2011 Miss E.Bouchard and Miss G.Min
Miss A.Dechaume and Miss E.Derly	*Miss D.Bedanova and Miss M.E.Salerni*	*Miss D.Schuurs and Miss H.C.Tang*
1989 Miss J.M.Capriati and Miss M.J.McGrath	2001 Miss G.Dulko and Miss A.Harkleroad	2012 Miss E.Bouchard and Miss T.Townsend
Miss A.Strnadova and Miss E.Sviglerova	*Miss C.Horiatopoulos and Miss B.Mattek*	*Miss B.Bencic and Miss A.Konjuh*
1990 Miss K.Habsudova and Miss A.Strnadova	2002 Miss E.Clijsters and Miss B.Strycova	2013 Miss B.Krejcikova and Miss K.Siniakova
Miss N.J.Pratt and Miss K.Sharpe	*Miss A.Baker and Miss A-L.Groenefeld*	*Miss A.Kalinina and Miss I.Shymanovich*
1991 Miss C.Barclay and Miss L.Zaltz	2003 Miss A.Kleybanova and Miss S.Mirza	2014 Miss T.Grende and Miss Q.Ye
Miss J.Limmer and Miss A.Woolcock	*Miss K.Bohmova and Miss M.Krajicek*	*Miss M.Bouzkova and Miss D.Galfi*
1992 Miss M.Avotins and Miss L.McShea	2004 Miss V.A.Azarenka and Miss V.Havartsova	2015 Miss D.Galfi and Miss F.Stollar
Miss P.Nelson and Miss J.Steven	*Miss M.Erakovic and Miss M.Niculescu*	*Miss V.Lapko and Miss T.Mihalikova*
1993 Miss L.Courtois and Miss N.Feber		2016 Miss U.M.Arconada and Miss C.Liu
Miss H.Mochizuki and Miss Y.Yoshida		*Miss M.Bolkvadze and Miss C.McNally*

GENTLEMEN'S WHEELCHAIR SINGLES

2016 G.Reid
S.Olsson

GENTLEMEN'S WHEELCHAIR DOUBLES

2006 S.Saida and S.Kunieda
M.Jeremiasz and J.Mistry

2007 R.Ammerlaan and R.Vink
S.Kunieda and S.Saida

2008 R.Ammerlaan and R.Vink
S.Houdet and N.Peifer

2009 S.Houdet and M.Jeremiasz
R.Ammerlaan and S.Kunieda

2010 R.Ammerlaan and S.Olsson
S.Houdet and S.Kunieda

2011 M.Scheffers and R.Vink
S.Houdet and M.Jeremiasz

2012 T.Egberink and M.Jeremiasz
R.Ammerlaan and R.Vink

2013 S.Houdet and S.Kunieda
F.Cattaneo and R.Vink

2014 S.Houdet and S.Kunieda
M.Scheffers and R.Vink

2015 G.Fernandez and N.Peifer
M.Jeremiasz and G.Reid

2016 A.T.Hewett and G.Reid
S.Houdet and N.Peifer

LADIES' WHEELCHAIR SINGLES

2016 Miss J.Griffioen
Miss A.van Koot

LADIES' WHEELCHAIR DOUBLES

2009 Miss K.Homan and Miss E.M.Vergeer
Miss D.Di Toro and Miss L.Shuker

2010 Miss E.M.Vergeer and Miss S.Walraven
Miss D.Di Toro and Miss L.Shuker

2011 Miss E.M.Vergeer and Miss S.Walraven
Miss J.Griffioen and Miss A.van Koot

2012 Miss J.Griffioen and Miss A.van Koot
Miss L.Shuker and Miss J.J.Whiley

2013 Miss J.Griffioen and Miss A.van Koot
Miss Y.Kamiji and Miss J.J.Whiley

2014 Miss Y.Kamiji and Miss J.J.Whiley
Miss J.Griffioen and Miss A.van Koot

2015 Miss Y.Kamiji and Miss J.J.Whiley
Miss J.Griffioen and Miss A.van Koot

2016 Miss Y.Kamiji and Miss J.J.Whiley
Miss J.Griffioen and Miss A.van Koot